upper-intermediate

second editi

teacher's book

Innovations

a course in natural English

Hugh Dellar   Darryl Hocking   Andrew Walkley
with Richard Moore

THOMSON
HEINLE

United Kingdom • United States • Australia • Canada • Mexico • Singapore • Spain

Innovations Upper-Intermediate
Teacher's Book
Second Edition
Dellar/Hocking/Walkley/Moore

Publisher: *Christopher Wenger*
Series Editor: *Jimmie Hill*
Editorial Manager: *Howard Middle/HM ELT Services*
Director of Marketing, ESL/ELT: *Amy Mabley*
Director of Development, ESL/ELT: *Anita Raducanu*
Developmental Editor: *Paul MacIntyre*
Editorial Assistant: *Christine Galvin*
Sr. Production Editor: *Sally Cogliano*

Associate Marketing Manager: *Laura Needham*
Sr. Print Buyer: *Mary Beth Hennebury*
Compositor: *Process ELT (www.process-elt.com)*
Production Management: *Process ELT*
Copyeditor: *Process ELT*
Cover/Text Designer: *Studio Image & Photographic Art
(www.studio-image.com)*
Printer: *Seng Lee Press*

Printed in Singapore.
1 2 3 4 5 6 7 8 9 10 07 06 05 04 03

For more information contact Thomson Learning, High Holborn
House, 50/51 Bedford Row, London WC1R 4LR United Kingdom
or Heinle, 25 Thomson Place, Boston, MA 02210 USA. You can visit
our Web site at http://www.heinle.com

For permission to use material from this text or
product, submit a request online at:
www.thomsonrights.com

ISBN: 0-7593-9849-6
(Teacher's Book)

Contents

Introduction

Innovations, first published in 2000, was created to provide intermediate to high-intermediate students with interesting models of natural spoken English to motivate them beyond the intermediate plateau. *Innovations* has now been updated and expanded into a new three-level series *(pre-intermediate, intermediate, upper-intermediate)* for classes looking for a fresh approach. It is based on a language-rich, lexical/grammatical syllabus that starts with the kinds of natural conversations that learners want to have.

What's so innovative about *Innovations*?

Innovations upper-intermediate, like the rest of the *Innovations* series, sets out to maximise students' ability to speak English fluently and to be able to understand natural spoken English. It does this not simply by providing students with plenty of opportunities to use language in personal, creative and communicative contexts, but more importantly, by providing a predominantly spoken model of English. The English presented in the whole *Innovations* series is the English commonly used in everyday life by native speakers. The series syllabus is designed to meet students' communicative needs. At all levels, the prime concern is what students will be able to *say* afterwards. As a result, the starting point for our syllabus is not the usual list of tense-based structures, but rather the typical kinds of conversations we believe students want to be able to have in English. What is then presented and practised is the language (both vocabulary and grammar) that will enable them to have those conversations.

How does *Innovations upper-intermediate* fit in with the rest of the series?

In the interest of retaining students' interest and encouraging their further language development, *Innovations upper-intermediate* does not simply repeat the same core tense structures which are focused on in *Innovations intermediate*. Many key structures are recycled and contrasted, but *Innovations upper-intermediate* also has a broader concept of grammar than many other courses at the same level. The Coursebook presents many features and patterns of spoken grammar. It clearly highlights these features and provides clear explanations and examples, as well as both controlled and freer practice activities.

In terms of vocabulary, *Innovations upper-intermediate* offers an increased focus on common fixed phrases and idioms, and extensive coverage of various interesting topics. It also continues the strong focus of the whole series on collocation. It shows students how words work in action with other words, and how conversation works in normal, everyday contexts.

Because of this consistent focus on presenting language as it is used, both grammar and vocabulary recur from unit to unit, and also across levels. This gives students the time and repeated exposure they need to learn language.

Organisation

Innovations upper-intermediate is divided into twenty units. Each unit is further divided into three two-page spreads, all of which provide self-contained and coherent lessons of 70–90 minutes, although obviously you may wish to alter these to suit your needs. All the units contain sections on using vocabulary and using grammar, as well as many speaking tasks.

The odd-numbered units contain a dialogue as the main source of language input. This dialogue is used first for general listening comprehension and then for detailed listening for the kinds of specific words and phrases that constitute important features of spoken English. The content of the dialogue is the basis for many of the speaking and language exercises within the unit.

The even-numbered units contain a reading text as the main source of input. Each reading text is followed by comprehension questions, vocabulary work and discussion of the topic. Each unit provides around six hours of work.

There is a **Review** after every four units.

*   The **Tapescript** at the back of the Coursebook features all of the dialogues, with the missing words and phrases highlighted in colour for easier identification.

*   The **Grammar commentary** at the back of the Coursebook provides notes on the grammar presented in the course.

*   The **Expression organiser** at the back of the Coursebook allows students to record and translate some of the most important expressions in each unit.

Other components

The Coursebook is complemented by a set of two Audio CDs/Audio Tapes, a Workbook, this Teacher's Book, and a separate, photocopiable Teacher's Resource Book. There is also support in the form of a website with useful links, and the test-creating program ExamView® Pro.

- **Audio CDs/Audio Tapes**
  The Audio CDs/Audio Tapes contain recordings of all the dialogues and reading texts, pronunciation exercises and those lexical exercises where stress and intonation are the main focus.

- **Workbook**
  The Workbook is for self-study, but any of the exercises in it may be done either in class or as homework. In addition, the Workbook contains writing tasks. Some of the Workbook exercises are directly related to activities in the Coursebook, making them useful for setting as homework, while others are more loosely connected and are designed to extend and expand students' knowledge of the language. If you choose not to use the Workbook in class, it is a good idea to recommend it to students as additional practice.

- **Teacher's Resource Book**
  The Teacher's Resource Book provides forty photocopiable activities and games which closely support the material in the Coursebook.

Getting the most out of *Innovations*

This Teacher's Book provides plenty of detailed advice on how to get the most out of *Innovations upper-intermediate*. However, there are some general points to make about the special features you will find in *Innovations upper-intermediate Coursebook*. These features are highlighted in the section that follows.

Features of Innovations

Using vocabulary

Throughout *Innovations upper-intermediate Coursebook* there are sections explicitly dealing with vocabulary. The tasks in these sections focus on collocations, idioms and other expressions related to the overall themes of the units. As you go through the answers, you can also get students to repeat the key language for pronunciation, and ask the kinds of questions we mention in the section below, **Noticing surrounding language**. The notes in the Teacher's Book will help you with this. The vocabulary exercises are followed by opportunities for students to use some of the language in short speaking tasks.

Using grammar

Each unit contains at least one section dealing with a particular grammatical structure. These structures range from the traditional tense-based structures like the present simple and present continuous to other less commonly looked-at structures like ways of emphasising by starting with *What*. The structures are always given in meaningful contexts, and students see how they can use the language themselves. Give students the basic patterns for the structure and encourage them to record examples from the exercises in their notebooks. Again, there are speaking tasks linked to the particular structure. Reference is always made to the corresponding section in the **Grammar commentary** section at the back of the Coursebook.

Noticing surrounding language

Although grammar exercises are provided primarily to focus on particular structures, we have presented all such language in natural contexts. This means that the surrounding language is just as important as the language being more explicitly focused on. If the exercise concerns the present perfect, do not miss the opportunity to point out other surrounding common phrases and expressions at the same time. One of the most important ways students will improve on their own is if they notice more. Turn 'noticing' into a major classroom activity. In order to do this, you need to not only explain meaning, but also ask students questions such as:

What other things can you ... ?

What other things can you describe as ... ?

What's the opposite of ... ?

What's the positive/negative way of saying ... ?

If you do ... , what would you do next/what happened before?

Where would you ... ?

What do you use a ... for?

What would you reply if someone said ... ?

The aim of these questions is to generate useful language connected to the word or expression in the exercise and also for students to get an idea of the limits of collocations and differences with their own LI. Asking questions like these is better than simply explaining, for three reasons. Firstly, they allow you to check whether students have understood what you explained. Secondly, they are more engaging for the students as you are involving them in the teaching process and accessing their current knowledge. Thirdly, they provide opportunities for students to extend their knowledge by introducing new language. In some ways, the questions are also convenient for you as a teacher, because students provide meanings in attempting answers and you can then provide the actual language by correcting any mistakes or re-stating what they said in more natural English. This new language can also be put on the board, ideally in the form of whole expressions as you would use them in speech.

You may also like to follow up a section of teaching like this by asking students to briefly personalise any new vocabulary you put on the board. For example, you could ask:

Do you know or have you heard about anyone who ... ?

Do you know or have you heard about anyone who has ... ?

When's the last time you ... ? Where? What happened?

Can you use any of these words/phrases/expressions to describe things in your life?

Which is the most useful word/phrase/expression?

Which words/phrases/expressions do you like most?

You could put students into pairs to do this kind of exercise for five or ten minutes. This is a good way of breaking up the lesson and getting away from the Coursebook for a moment. It also encourages students to get to know each other better and, unlike supplementary materials, requires little planning and no fighting with the photocopier!

The teacher's notes often suggest questions you can ask about language in the texts and there are also good examples of these kinds of questions in the **Vocabulary quizzes** in the **Review** units. It may take a little time to get used to this style of teaching, and students also may initially need to get used to it, but it is worth persisting with it, as it produces a dynamic and language-rich classroom.

Grammar commentary

The **Grammar commentary** starts on page 159 of the Coursebook and begins with two pages outlining the basic approach to grammar taken in the book. Ask students to read these pages early on in the course and discuss any questions that arise from it. The grammar points that follow refer to the **Using grammar** sections within the units. Generally, you can ask students to read the **Grammar commentary** as a way to review the language after they have looked at particular structures. However, in some cases you might want students to come up with a guideline or 'rule' themselves and then compare it to the explanation in the **Grammar commentary** before working on the exercises. The **Grammar commentary** is also another good source of useful examples for students to record.

Dialogues

The dialogues form the main input in each of the odd-numbered units. They are based on corpora of spoken English, but have been modified to avoid the redundancy, overlapping and false starts common in everyday speech. However, they do still retain many other useful features of such speech. The dialogues are examples of typical conversations that people have about everyday topics and contain many commonly-used phrases and expressions.

When using the dialogues in class, play the recording once so students can answer the gist questions in **While you listen**, and then once more to allow them to identify the words and phrases which complete the gaps. If your students find this hard, play the recording a third time and pause after each gap to give them more time to write. Finally, play the recording one last time as students silently read the dialogue. Listening to natural spoken English whilst also reading what they are hearing helps students get used to the way language is 'chunked': where speakers pause, and – more importantly – where they do not pause. It also helps students notice other features of everyday speech, such as discourse markers like *Oh, Well, Now, Then*. You could follow up by getting students to read the dialogue aloud in pairs – either the whole dialogue or just part of it.

Much of the language presented and explored in the units appears in the dialogues, so students get to see and hear it in meaningful contexts. For example, in the dialogue **The Brother from Hell** on page 10, Simon describes his brother as *a bit old-fashioned*, *a bit traditional*, which is an example of one of the modifiers from the **Using grammar** section on page 9.

Reading texts

Reading texts form the main input in the even-numbered units. These texts are derived from authentic articles, but have been re-written to include maximally useful vocabulary and collocations. The texts are also all designed to elicit some kind of personal response from students, whether it be laughter, disbelief or shock!

Encourage students to read the whole text through without worrying too much about any words they don't know. Tell them to put their pens down for a minute and relax! One good way of ensuring they do this is to play the recording as they read it the first time or, if you want a slower pace, to read it out yourself. Important vocabulary is focused on later, and students need to gain confidence in their ability to understand most – if not all – of a text. Encourage students to focus on the many words they *do* know!

Each reading text is followed by a speaking task where students have the opportunity to react personally to the text and to extend the discussion on a related theme. This can either be done in pairs or in small groups. There are also exercises that focus on particular lexical items or collocations within the text.

Encourage students to re-read the text, finding other interesting expressions and collocations. One question that you can ask is if anyone found a collocation that was surprising or unusual. For example, in **Surprise For Jailbird Dad** in Unit 2, students might find *a great big hug* a surprising collocation. Suggest that students use a good English–English dictionary, not only to check the meaning of words but also to read the examples, which often contain useful collocations and phrases.

With both the reading and the listening texts, you could simply ask students: *Do you have any questions about the text?* Note that this a different question to *Are there any words which you don't know?*, because it allows students to ask about anything. They can ask about words they *do* know, but which may appear with a new meaning or in a new collocation; they can ask about expressions; they can ask about content; they can even ask you what *you* think!

Encouraging students to ask questions is a good way to encourage them to notice language. It also helps to create a good relationship between students and teacher.

Extra reading texts

Several of the units have smaller reading texts, for example **Full-Time Job!** on page 12, which are related to the overall theme of the unit. These reading texts are mainly for fun and lead in to fluency work through discussion in the speaking tasks that follow. Although the prime focus of these texts is not explicit vocabulary work, they have been written to include useful vocabulary, and provide another opportunity to point out particular collocations and expressions within the texts.

Speaking tasks

There are speaking tasks throughout the Coursebook. These are intended both as a way of encouraging students to use some of the new language that they have met, in personalised ways, and also as an opportunity for students to relax and enjoy talking to each other! Whenever possible, try to introduce these speaking tasks by talking about yourself and encouraging the class to ask you questions. This serves as a model of what you are asking students to do and is another good source of language input. Also, students generally like finding out more about their teachers.

You may wish to use these discussion periods as a chance to monitor students' spoken performance and to gather student errors to focus on later, or as a chance to listen for gaps in students' vocabularies which can later be addressed. A good way to give feedback on these sections is to re-tell what one or two students said. Re-telling what students say – sometimes called reformulation – is a good technique because it allows even the weakest students to share their experiences and ideas with the whole class without the pressure of performing in front of them. It's quicker – there are no painful pauses – and maintains the pace of the lesson. Finally, it allows you to correct and introduce useful new language in a way which acknowledges that the student has successfully conveyed his/her meaning. You can write some of this new language on the board if you like, but it's not strictly necessary. Sometimes you may wish to just take a back seat and have no feedback.

Pronunciation

As *Innovations* places such an emphasis on spoken English, pronunciation is given a high priority throughout the series. The recording provides models of many short dialogues, language patterns and expressions. The recording can be used to help students practise the expressions. Students should be encouraged to repeat the expressions several times, both chorally and individually, until they can say them relatively naturally. It is important that students do not just learn forms and meanings, but also learn how whole phrases and expressions are said by fluent speakers.

Real English notes

The Real English notes throughout the Coursebook refer to a particular piece of language – a word, phrase or grammatical structure – that appears in one of the tasks. The notes contain features of everyday English which many more traditional coursebooks overlook, and so it is important to draw students' attention to the explanations and examples. Add more examples or ask a few related questions to exploit the notes further, if you wish. In the **Review** units, language from these notes is recycled in different contexts.

Jokes

In some of the units there are jokes, partly to bring some light relief and extra humour into the class, and partly because being able to tell jokes is an important part of daily life. Students practise telling jokes, and focus on the pausing, stress and intonation that make a good joke-teller.

Review units

There is a **Review** after every four units. This gives students the chance to revisit and consolidate language they have studied. These **Reviews** have been written with additional speaking exercises to use in class time. There are also **Look back and check** and **What can you remember?** exercises, where students repeat and recall information they have learned. Repeating activities, perhaps unsurprisingly, often leads to better student performance the second time around and you may want to do these exercises more regularly as a quick way of revising things. The **Vocabulary quizzes** are best done in pairs or groups or even with the whole class divided into two teams. You could even award points and score it as if it was a TV quiz show!

Finally, the last section of the **Review**, **Learner advice**, provides a short text which relates our own experiences as teachers and our ideas on how to improve students' learning strategies. This is treated as a normal reading text with pre- and post-reading tasks, where students reflect on their own practice and our advice.

Tapescript

The **Tapescript** starts on page 148 and features all of the dialogues, with missing words and phrases highlighted in colour for easier identification. As well as the dialogues and short listening texts, many of the language practice activities are also on the recording.

Photographs

Photographs play an important role throughout the Coursebook, and many exercises ask students very specifically to describe photos (e.g. page 18), to role-play situations depicted in them (e.g. page 47) or to respond personally to them (e.g. page 53). Ideas about how to use photos like this are generally given in the explanation of the task, but additional ways to exploit the photos are given in individual unit notes in the Teacher's Book.

Because *Innovations upper-intermediate* is so rich in interesting visuals, the pictures can be used to do activities not directly related to the Coursebook. For example, you may be working through Unit 16, but there is nothing to stop you using the photo on page 120 to set up a role play between a traffic warden and a driver in your afternoon class, or to use the wedding photo on page 110 to set up a debate on getting married or just living together.

Language strips

Language strips as a resource

The language strips at the beginning of each unit provide valuable input which can be exploited in many different ways. They are particularly useful as a source of five-minute filler activities, between more substantial activities or at the end of a lesson. You should not, however, try to explain all the language in the strip. Instead, try to ensure students notice and learn two or three expressions from each strip.

The language in the language strips

All the expressions are correct, natural spoken language, including idioms, fixed expressions and expressions containing phrasal verbs. Often, there are also some more colloquial topic-specific expressions connected to something mentioned in the unit. The language in the language strips is useful for all students, but particularly those who have had less chance to use their English in 'real' situations. Point out that many of the expressions, usually those which contain the word *I*, are useful in talking about yourself, your opinions and reactions. The notes for each unit give definitions and examples of some of the more idiomatic expressions.

You may need to give some guidance about how students can find out about these expressions. For some of the more idiomatic ones, for example, *I really get a kick out of it* in Unit 3, tell students to look at the phrases at the end of the dictionary entry for the key word, in this case, *kick*. If students are studying in an English-speaking country, you could also encourage them to go out and ask people about the expressions.

Using the language strips

Students could look at the language strips on their own, but they are probably best used for pair or small-group activities in class. Ask students to look through the language strips, choose some expressions that look interesting and to find out more about them. They can share their information in small groups in a later class. They could then do another activity related to the language strip. The notes for each unit give specific questions you can ask, but the following are some general ideas which can be used for most of the language strips:

1. Ask students to find the expressions:
    a. which are responses to two or three questions or remarks you write on the board.
    b. which express very neatly a complicated idea you would otherwise express in a roundabout way. For example, in Unit 8: *It's too early to go home. There is so much more we can do. The night is young.*

2. Copy some of the expressions onto an overhead transparency, leaving some gaps. Ask students to complete the expressions before opening their Coursebooks, and then compare their answers with the expressions in the language strip.

3. Ask students to identify expressions:
    a. which contain a familiar idiom.
    b. which contain expressions with a phrasal verb.
    c. which contain language which has occurred in an earlier unit, such as modifiers or softeners, for example, *a bit of a, just,* etc.

4. Ask students to sort the expressions in different ways:
    a. positive vs. negative expressions.
    b. formal vs. informal expressions.
    c. those which are more likely to be used by men/women.
    d. those more likely to be used by young/older people.
    e. remarks which initiate a conversation vs. responses.
    f. (perhaps most importantly) those they would like to use themselves vs. expressions they would not feel comfortable using.

The pictures and language strips provide ways of introducing the topic and some of the language relevant to the unit.

Recording language

It is a good idea to help students organise a notebook to record the language they meet. Early on in the course, talk about recording this language in an organised way and suggest a notebook divided into several sections:

*   a section organised alphabetically, containing not only the target words but associated collocations and phrases

*   a section organised around themes such as describing people, work, films, etc.

*   a section organised around 'delexicalised' verbs and nouns such as *get, take, point, thing*; a section for phrasal verbs

*   a section for idioms; and a section for grammatical patterns and structures such as the present continuous and *was/were going to … but …* .

Also talk about what should be recorded. Instead of just isolated words, encourage the recording of complete phrases, collocations and even question/response exchanges. The Coursebook is a great resource of useful contextualised language that can be transferred directly to students' notebooks. Tell students to translate these larger expressions and idioms into an equivalent in their own language.

1 Talking about people

Unit overview

General topic
Describing friends and family, and talking about what they do.

Dialogue
Melanie and Simon talk about their families.

Reading
The Pridham family are expecting their twentieth child!

Language input
- Adjectives to describe people's appearance and character: *good-looking, going grey, moody, amusing*, etc.
- Modifiers: *really nice, quite creative, a bit boring, a bit of a moaner, a bit too nice*, etc.
- Positive and negative adjectives: *tidy, messy*, etc.
- Contrasting present tenses (present simple and present continuous): *He usually works in the centre of town, but this week he's working from home.*

Language strip

Draw students' attention to the expressions in the language strip. Ask them to look quickly through the expressions and choose three they are curious about. For the next class meeting, they should find out about the meaning and usage of their chosen expressions. Good resources are print or online dictionaries or, even better, proficient English speakers. Demonstrate how to find one of the expressions in a dictionary by choosing a key word. For example, for *Well, he does take after his father*, look under *take*. In the next class, students share what they have learned. You could also ask them to find expressions in the strip that describe a person's appearance or those that describe personality. Encourage them to add any expressions they think are useful to their notebooks or the **Expression organiser** on page 167. You might need to explain some of the more idiomatic expressions in the strip:

- If someone *is a real laugh*, it means they are fun to be with.
- If someone is *a bottle blonde*, it means they dye their hair blonde.
- *PC* stands for *politically correct*. If you want to be PC, you try to use language that doesn't offend and is fair to all people regardless of race, gender, age, physical ability or sexual orientation. For example, it is considered PC to say *chairperson*, rather than *chairman*.

- If you *fancy someone*, it means that you are sexually attracted to them. If you *don't go for redheads*, it means you don't usually fancy people with red hair.
- If someone *wouldn't say boo to a goose*, it means they are very timid.
- If you *hear something on the grapevine*, it means that you hear some news from friends or colleagues rather than in an official announcement.
- If you say *she's a friend of a friend of mine*, it means she is your friend's friend.

Using vocabulary

1 Describing people

Model the task for the students by choosing three of your friends or family (or yourself), and choosing the best expressions to describe them. Afterwards, ask if anyone can recall any of the expressions they heard. Choose a couple of examples and write them on the board to illustrate how they are used. For example: *She's got fair hair. She's a bit on the short side.*

Ask the class to suggest three or four more examples that can follow *she's got/she has …* (e.g. *darkish hair, a good sense of humour*) and three or four that can follow *she's …* (e.g. *energetic, going grey*). Get students to talk about the people they chose. Encourage them to ask their partners further questions. You could also explore the use of the suffix *-ish*, which can often be added to adjectives describing appearance. It gives the meaning of *partly, to a certain degree* (in contrast to *completely*). For example:
She's got reddish hair. She's tallish.

Ask the class to tell you to which adjectives in the list they think *-ish* can be added. Possibilities include *fairish, whitish, greyish, baldish, youngish, tallish*.

2 Speaking

The questions provide a follow-up to **1 Describing people**. This would work well in a small group discussion. You might want to talk about the word *features*, explaining that it usually describes the face and is often used in the plural form. Give some examples:
She's got delicate features.
My mouth is one of my best features.

3 Who's who?

Before the students listen to the recording, ask for expressions (including any from the list in **1 Describing people**) to describe each of the people in the four photos. Tell the students they can consult you, a dictionary, or each other for ideas. For example:
The man in picture one looks like he's in his thirties.

Ask what kind of personality they think each of the people has. For example:
I think the woman in picture two is probably very easy-going.

Tell them to listen and then discuss their answers with a partner, and then to recall any useful expressions they heard. Write them on the board. Some that you may want to point out are:
He's got a great sense of humour (ask for other adjectives that could be used instead of *great*).

She's a really energetic sort of person (ask for other adjectives that can fit in this pattern).

She's got a very warm personality (ask how you would express the opposite).

Replay the recording so that they can hear the phrases again. Encourage students to record the phrases that they like in their notebooks.

Answers

Picture 1 is Nick; Picture 2 is Kirsty;
Picture 3 is Matt; Picture 4 is Jenny.

Photo opportunity

The photographs on page 8 provide good opportunities for discussion. You could use the ideas here at any time during the unit. Here are some possibilities:

- Ask students to discuss if any of the people remind them of anyone they know or have met, and in what way. Feed in language to help them. For example: *This girl looks a bit like a German friend of mine. This man reminds me a bit of my uncle.*

- Ask students to guess how old each person is and what they do. Feed in useful structures if needed. For example: *The man with the glasses looks about twenty-five. This girl must be in her early twenties. She might be a fashion student or something like that.*

- Ask students to discuss whether or not they've ever – or would ever – dress like the people in the pictures or have their hair like that. Ask the class to discuss why/why not, and to give extra details where possible.

- Ask each person to invent the personality and/or life story for one of the people. For example: *She's a very bad-tempered sort of person. She never used to be this way, though. It all started when her daughter decided to marry someone much older.* Students can then share their ideas in pairs.

Using grammar

1 Modifiers

Go over the short explanation of modifiers, mentioning how some are useful in 'softening' comments. For example, *This is a bit boring* is more acceptable than *This is boring.* Model the exercise yourself and/or elicit from the class one or two words for each pattern before asking students to complete the task.

Answers

Possible answers:

1. moody … pleasant, difficult … easy-going (point out the contrasting adjectives)
2. annoying, nice, pleasant, funny
3. narrow-minded, conservative
4. nut, snob
5. generous, sarcastic

Encourage students to find out more about the people their partners described. Refer them to the **Grammar commentary, G1 Modifiers** on page 159.

2 Pronunciation

This use of *quite* is common in British English, but the difference in meaning can be difficult for learners to discern. As an introduction, you could write *Your essay was quite good* on the board and ask the class if they would be pleased if they received that comment. Without hearing it, we wouldn't know if it meant it was just OK or if it was really good. Go through the explanation, saying the examples several times. Ask the class to identify what is done to the voice to indicate stress. (The stressed word or syllable is spoken with a higher pitch, is longer, clearer and sometimes a little louder.) After students have listened to the recording and repeated the sentences, explain that the context helps make the meanings clear. For example:
A: How are you getting home?
B: Walking. I live quite <u>near</u> the office.
A: That's nice. I hate driving in to work.

A: Do you ever walk home?
B: Well, I live <u>quite</u> near the office, but a bit too far to walk.
A: Oh, do you want a lift, then?

As an extension, get pairs of students to construct their own dialogue for one of the examples and perform it for other members of the class.

3 Speaking

Read through the questions so that the students can hear the expressions. Use the picture to help with any vocabulary such as *body-piercing* and *tattoos*. For *a pain in the neck* refer students to the **Real English** note. This expression can sometimes be shortened to *a pain*. For example:

My mother can be a bit of a pain sometimes.
Parking is a real pain.

Ask the students to tell you what or who they find *a pain (in the neck)*. Get them to work through the questions individually first, and then to discuss their opinions in pairs or in small groups. You can then bring the whole class together to share ideas. This is a great chance for the class to let off a bit of steam! Try to remain impartial yourself. Remind them to look at the questions again and to underline the modifiers.

Photo opportunity

Ask the class to describe what they can see in the picture on page 9. Feed in relevant vocabulary, such as *He's got tattoos all over his face*. Make sure you give the class whole phrases, not just isolated words such as *tattoos*. The picture can then be used to encourage debate on why people feel the need to have tattoos and piercings, whether they suit some people or not, whether anyone in the class has, or would have, any done. Alternatively, students could prepare a role play between a teenager who wants to get their face pierced and a tattoo on their arm, and a concerned parent. Divide the class into two groups – a parent group and a teenager group – and give them five minutes to plan what they are going to say, what line of argument they are going to follow. Brainstorm a list of useful phrases beforehand to give each group. For example:

All my friends have got them.
I can always take it out if I get sick of it.
It might go septic.
You'll be stuck with it for life.

Feed in vocabulary where necessary. You could also prepare a list on a handout or transparency of twenty possible things that might be said between parent and child, and ask the class to decide which were said by the parent and which by the teenager.

4 Friends and relatives

This task focuses on expressions to describe relationships. Ask the class if they have similar expressions in their own languages and whether they agree with the ones here. Make sure that students hear how the expressions are said, particularly number 8, where *of* is stressed. Ask questions to check on the meanings and to generate other collocations. Some examples could be:

- If you *know someone by sight*, would you recognise them if you saw them? Would you have a long conversation with them?

- Do we use *his/her ex* to just refer to former husbands and wives? How about girlfriends/ boyfriends?

- If someone introduced you to their *partner*, would they be married? Would they be friends?

- If you *know of someone*, you've heard people talking about them. What are other expressions with *know of*? (*Are we finishing early today? Not that I know of.*)

Talk about some of the examples yourself before getting students to talk in pairs. You could also try and recycle some of the language from the unit as you do so. It is very important for students to hear this kind of controlled, recycling teacher-talk.

Listening

1 Before you listen

Start off by talking about your family or asking the class to ask you questions about the people. This provides a model for the students so they can talk to a partner about their family.

2 While you listen (The Brother from Hell!)

Talk about the expression *Simon's popped in to Melanie's house*. Ask whether students think this means Simon is going to stay long. Explain that you can also *pop into a shop for a loaf of bread* or *pop into the café for a bite to eat*. (Refer them to the **Real English** note for an explanation of the expression *the brother from hell*.) Tell the students not to try to understand every word in the text, but only to try to answer the two questions. Make sure they cover the text the first time you play the recording. Play it twice if necessary, then check the answers to the two questions.

Answers

1. Melanie's an only child; Simon's got an older brother and a younger sister.
2. Melanie gets on well with her mum, but she doesn't really get on with her dad. Simon gets on well with his sister, but not so well with his brother.

Now explain the second task. First, see if students can fill in the first two or three gaps from memory with a partner. Play the recording again for students to fill in the missing words. Pause the recording so they have time to write in what they hear. Finally, play the recording again with students listening while reading the tapescript on page 148. The missing words are in blue. You may want students to read the dialogue, or part of it, in pairs. Don't be afraid to ask them to listen several times. The more they listen to natural spoken English, the more chance they have of acquiring that language and improving their own performance.

Answer questions about any of the gapped expressions/ words by giving examples and collocations. For example:

- If you *do temping work*, you aren't working as a full-time permanent employee of a company. Often you work for a *temping agency*.

- If you *steer clear of a topic*, you avoid talking about it. You can also *steer clear of an area* or *a person*.

The conversation contains many other useful expressions and collocations. Encourage students to find, ask about and record in their notebooks any they find interesting or unusual. You could also exploit the conversation in another way by asking them to find expressions with *talk*, *say* and *tell* (e.g. *I just don't have anything to say to him. You mean you can't tell? You haven't really talked about them very much. Oh, there's not much to tell, really*) and discussing the differences in how each is used.

3 | Speaking

Discuss these questions in small groups, giving students a chance to use some of the expressions covered so far.

Using vocabulary

1 | Adjectives

Before students mark the adjectives positive or negative, choose one, *talkative*, for example. Ask: *If someone described you as talkative, would you be pleased or not?* Stress the subjective nature of most adjectives describing personality and that there are no correct answers, though obviously certain words, like *messy*, are more commonly used negatively, while others, like *sensible*, are generally positive. You may need to explain *conservative* and *liberal*.

- If someone is *conservative*, they don't like things that aren't seen as being 'normal' or 'traditional'. For example, if you *dress conservatively*, you wouldn't wear shorts and a T-shirt to the office. Would you describe *the brother from hell* as having *conservative views*?

- If someone is *liberal*, they are more easy-going in their views and more willing to accept changes. For example, if you have a *liberal attitude to* marriage, you might allow your daughter to live with her partner before getting married.

To do the stress task, allow students to hear each of the adjectives in the context of a simple phrase such as *People often tell me I'm ... .* Having the adjective at the end like this ensures that the word itself is stressed.

Answers

religious   tra<u>di</u>tional   <u>qui</u>et   <u>talk</u>ative   <u>ti</u>dy
laid-<u>back</u>   con<u>ser</u>vative   am<u>bi</u>tious   <u>strict</u>
business-<u>mind</u>ed (or business-minded)   indi<u>vid</u>ual
<u>mess</u>y   <u>lib</u>eral   hard-<u>work</u>ing   <u>sen</u>sible

Get the class to choose adjectives from the list in this exercise, from the list on page 8, or any others they want for the list of four most positive and negative adjectives. Get them to explain their choices to a partner.

2 | Judging by appearances

The photos provide a good opportunity to use some of the adjectives covered in the unit along with appropriate modifiers. Write a few sentence starters on the board. For example:
She looks a bit ... .
She looks like the kind of person who ... .

Get students to talk about the pictures in pairs.

3 | Emphasising

This activity encourages students to describe things more fluently by repeating adverbs and using synonyms. Remember students may need to listen and repeat several times. Use the pictures to practise these structures. A fun way of extending the task is to ask students to think of things that the objects themselves might say, using two adjectives and the same adverb. For example, the shoe might say *Oh, no, look at her feet. They look really big and really smelly*, while the bear might say *Oh, this water is really nice, really warm*, or *How would you feel if I watched you having a bath?*

Get the class to underline the adjectives and adverbs in the conversation about Thailand as you read it aloud. Choose one of the descriptions to model yourself before asking the class to do it. Encourage students to ask you questions.

Reading

1 | Before you read

The pre-reading questions could be discussed in groups or as a class.

2 While you read (Full-time job!)

Explain to students that they should underline anything they find surprising in the text. You can check for comprehension by asking a couple of questions. For example:

What does Kevin Pridham do for a living?

How are the Pridhams going to deal with the problem of clothing all their children?

Encourage students to look for any interesting or useful expressions and collocations and record these in their notebooks. Here are some expressions you may want to point out:

- You usually *get pocket money* from your parents when you are a child and not working.
- As well as *going through loaves of bread,* you can also *go through clothing.* For example: *I go through two pairs of shoes a year.*
- If you *do odd jobs,* you do little things like the washing-up. For example: *I used to get £10 a week in pocket money for doing odd jobs around the house.*

3 Speaking

Use these discussion questions in small groups to allow the class to share their reactions to the text as well as practise some of the expressions.

Using grammar

1 Present tenses

You could introduce this exercise by talking about what your friends or family do for a living, or make up some fictitious relatives and occupations and ask the class to guess which are true and which aren't. For example:

My mother, Wendy, does a lot of work in television.

Talking about what you do for a living is a good example of when we typically use the present simple. The students will probably have come across this context many times. In the first task, however, the focus is also on some typical patterns like *I work in … , I do … work for … , I run a … business.* Point out that in spoken English, it is more common to use contracted forms with *be* in the present simple.

> **Answers**
>
> 1. am 2. works 3. is 4. work 5. works 6. work
> 7. is 8. 'is 9. is 10. do 11. does 12. is 13. work
> 14. runs

2 Speaking

Students may need help with vocabulary when trying to talk about jobs. Tell them not to worry if they can't say exactly what the jobs are. You can write up these examples as a guide:

He's a kind of businessman or something.

She runs some kind of import-export business.

After the students have finished the discussion, you could work on collocations by eliciting other adjectives that are used to describe *job,* for example, *well-paid/ tedious/challenging/worthwhile,* and asking: *Did you find out about anyone who has a challenging job?*

3 Grammar discussion

Tell students to discuss the sentences in pairs. All the a-sentences, with the present simple form, talk or ask about things the speaker sees as permanent, timeless facts, while the b-sentences, with the present continuous form, are all seen as being temporary, relating to particular periods of time. The time expressions used with the present continuous are *this month, at the moment, this weekend, at the moment,* and *again.* You could ask the class to write their own simple guidelines for explaining the different uses of these verb forms and then to look at the **Grammar commentary, G2 Present simple and present continuous** on page 159. They can then modify their guidelines as necessary. Make sure you draw students' attention to the fact that the present continuous is used with time expressions that make the temporary nature of the event described clear – *this month, at the moment,* and so on. The absence of time expressions for the present simple is because the events described are seen as generalisations. Make sure that students notice the modifiers in several of the examples too. You could also point out the pattern *I find my dad a bit dull,* or *I'm finding my job a bit boring.* Elicit other nouns and adjectives that could be used with this pattern. For example:

I find this city a bit expensive.

I'm finding this exercise a bit challenging.

4 Grammar in context

You might need to explain *left-wing* and *the socialist revolution* in question 5. You could make a comparison with *the brother form hell* on page 10. Refer students to the **Real English** note for *pretty.* As well as asking what they are *pretty good at,* you could write *I'm pretty …* on the board and then ask them to complete it in five different ways. For example:

I'm pretty tired at the moment.

I'm pretty sure she's pregnant.

Ask students to compare and discuss their answers in pairs, and then ask the whole class how they made their decisions and which other words helped them decide on the best verb form.

Answers

1. works, 's working, 's trying
2. 's acting, 's not normally/isn't normally
3. runs, 's looking after
4. don't talk, Don't you get on
5. 's, 's still waiting
6. aren't talking, 's still

Questions 7–9 personalise the context, and students should talk about their answers in small groups or pairs. Encourage them to choose four or five examples each of the present continuous and the present simple to record in their notebooks. They could put the continuous examples on one page and the simple form examples on another. Tell them that they should record as much of the surrounding language as possible.

5 Famous present tenses

This is an optional exercise. You can ask students to try to guess what the sayings mean and think of when they might be used. Number 2 is often quoted by the English about themselves. You could ask students what their impressions of English or British people are.

Answers

3. *What goes up must come down* is used in situations where you want to say that one thing inevitably follows another. For example, if someone is very annoyed, you know they will calm down eventually.
4. You use *an elephant never forgets* when you remember something that someone said or did to you that they would prefer you to forget.
5. You would say *it never rains, but it pours* when something bad has just happened to you – just after two or three other bad things have also happened.
6. If you tell someone they're *making a mountain out of a molehill*, you mean they're worrying too much about something that is really a very small problem.

 ## Expression organiser

Don't forget to introduce students to the **Expression organiser** on page 167.

Read the short introduction at the top of the page and ask the students to translate the expressions into their own language for homework or with a student with the same mother tongue. Emphasise how it is vital to translate the expression as a whole, not word for word. Tell them to spend time at home reading through the unit again and adding any other expressions they want to be able to use themselves.

2 Friends and relatives

Unit overview

General topic
Relatives, friends and relationships.

Reading
A criminal's son meets his father as an adult for the first time.

Language input
- Relationship and 'body' idioms: *We really are on the same wavelength, I bet it cost her an arm and a leg,* etc.
- Comparatives: *His dad is not as bad as the media make out, It's much easier to park,* etc.
- Pronunciation of the 'schwa': *It's much better than it used to be.*
- Phrasal verbs with *up: We'd better get up early, Cheer up!* etc.
- Giving bad news: *Oh, haven't you heard? I'm afraid not,* etc.

Language strip

Ask students to look quickly through the expressions in the language strip and select those that they are curious about. Tell them to find out as much as they can about their choices. In a later class, get them to share their findings in small groups. You can come back to the language strip while working through the unit and use it as a short filler. Ask questions like:

Which expressions seem to be negative?

Which expressions might be used if you were talking about someone you didn't fancy?

Here are some of the expressions your students might have difficulty with:

- You might say *I think she had it done in America* to talk about someone who has had plastic surgery.
- If you say you *wouldn't like to meet someone on a dark night,* you are implying that the person is really scary.
- If you *get on like a house on fire with someone,* it means that you quickly become really good friends. For example: *As soon as we met, we got on like a house on fire.*
- *Men with beards usually have weak chins* is a stereotype implying that people with weak chins also have a weak character and grow beards to hide the fact.
- If you say someone *has an old head on young shoulders,* you mean that they are wiser than you would expect for their age.

- If someone *has their head screwed on,* they are sensible.
- If you say that you wished someone would *pull their socks up,* you want them to work or try harder.

Lead in

Lead in to the theme of the unit and the reading text by asking students if they have ever met up with any distant relatives that they hadn't seen for ages. When? Where? What was it like? Have they got any other relatives that they have never met? Where?

Reading

1 Before you read

Use the questions to lead in to the topic of the reading text. You may need to go over the meaning, use and pronunciation of *infamous*. These questions could be discussed in small groups.

2 While you read (Surprise for Jailbird Dad)

Explain what the article is going to be about and set the students the goal of answering the three questions. Remind them that they do not need to understand every expression or word. Ask the class to share their answers in pairs or groups. Often students quote large chunks of text in answer to these kinds of questions. To move them away from this, tell them to cover the text while they are talking. Also, encourage them to share their overall reaction to the text. For example:
What did you find interesting/amusing/shocking?

Answers
1. He's spent a lot of time in prison because he keeps on taking hostages and attacking other prisoners.
2. Although it came as an initial shock when he found out, Michael wanted to meet his father. He felt good about meeting him. He said they got on like a house on fire.
3. Because Bronson was recently involved in another violent incident, he probably won't be coming out of prison soon. But Michael is still young and we don't know how old his father is, so it's still possible.

Students might wonder about a couple of cultural references.

- *Have a pint* means to go to the pub and have a beer. (You could even come up with alternatives such as *All I want to do is get home and have a cup of tea/have a bath/put my feet up/go to bed.*)
- If you say something *cost the taxpayer £60,000,* it means that the state provided the money for it.

Ask whether anyone noticed any interesting expressions and collocations in the reading text. Here are some that you might want to mention: *incredible physical strength, it came as a total shock, old habits die hard* (this is a fixed expression meaning *it's very difficult to give up either a good or bad habit*). Encourage students to record those expressions and collocations that they like in their notebooks.

3 Speaking

Use these follow-up questions to continue the discussion in small groups. Draw students' attention to the phrasal verb *lock up.* Give them other examples of nouns that can be locked up (*house, car*) and phrases like:
Remember to lock up before you leave.

This unit has a lot of examples of phrasal verbs, so keep pointing them out as you work your way through.

4 Vocabulary check

Tell students the relevant paragraph numbers if you want to speed up this activity. Note that these sentences are good definitions for the target words as they provide a meaning, a context, a typical pattern and usually a collocation. Point the following out: *take hostages, give … a hug, profits go to charity.*

Answers

1. reunited (paragraph 1)
2. burglary (paragraph 2)
3. hostage, hostages (paragraph 2)
4. infamous (paragraph 3)
5. hug (paragraph 4)
6. bushy (paragraph 5)
7. hold (paragraph 6)
8. charity (paragraph 6)

Here are some phrasal verbs and preposition phrases to point out too: *break into someone's home, put pressure on another country, famous for, carry out a plan, give away money.*

Using vocabulary

1 Idioms focus

Students are probably aware of traditional idioms such as *it's raining cats and dogs* and *kick the bucket.* This exercise, however, focuses on some idiomatic expressions that are probably more common and potentially more useful.

For sections 1 and 2, remember to give students the opportunity to hear how these idioms sound. You could have them check the answers in pairs with one person reading up to the blank or choice (*We simply don't see eye to … , My car's on its last …*) while the other person listens and says the missing word without looking at the Coursebook (*eye, legs*). Ask questions about the idioms so that students can hear different contexts. For example:
Who are you really close to in your family?
Would you say you're on the same wavelength as your parents?
Apart from your boss, who else could breathe down your neck?

Have the students translate the idioms into their first language. This can be done individually or in small groups depending on the make-up of your class. This is a good opportunity for them to see the benefit of translating chunks of language.

Answers

1. eye 2. moment 3. close 4. wavelength

2 Body idioms

A fun way to reinforce some of the body idioms is to have students make note cards. Tell them to write the idiom in English, a translation in their first language and the examples on one side of a blank note card. On the other side, they should draw a picture to help them remember the idiom. Demonstrate an example on the board. You could draw a person handing over an arm and a leg in payment for a brand new car. Tell them that their drawings don't have to be works of art. These note cards can be used later in a game to review these idiomatic expressions; for example, by looking at the picture, can they remember the idiom, or in monolingual classes, a translation. You could also have students make note cards like this for other expressions. After each unit, for example, they could choose ten expressions, make the note cards and add them to their stack. If they bring their stack of cards every day, you can always use them for quick 'filler' activities.

Answers

1. legs 2. leg 3. neck 4. foot 5. head 6. face 7. chest 8. eyes

3 | Speaking

The questions help the students hear and use some of the idiomatic expressions. If possible, talk about some personal experiences first. For example:
I really put my foot in it last weekend. I was sitting next to this woman on the bus and I asked her when her baby was due. It turned out she wasn't pregnant at all. I got off at the next stop.

Using grammar

1 | Comparatives: *not as ... as ...*

The examples in this exercise include some common expressions using the *not as … as …* pattern. You can have students check the answers in pairs, with one person reading the first half and the other person saying the second half. Give the class an opportunity to hear how the examples sound.

Answers
1. d.   2. c.   3. b.   4. f.   5. a.   6. e.

For the second task, tell students to add real names here, as well as adjectives or adverb phrases. Encourage them to give true examples, of people in their lives. Language is much easier to learn if it is connected to something in our own lives. Students should come to feel that they somehow own this new language. Model some answers yourself first and get the class to ask you questions. This will help when they talk about their own answers.

2 | Comparing the present with the past

Here comparative structures are put into a practical context. Go through the examples, letting the students hear how each sounds. Ask them to underline the parts where the comparison is being made (*it's much easier to park than the old one, it was much better going in May, it wasn't as hot as the last time, there were fewer tourists*). Draw their attention to how *much* can modify the comparative form to show the degree of difference. Have them complete the dialogues with the correct forms and then act them out.

Answers
1. more powerful
2. bigger, as dark
3. as good, more serious, more fun (*more fun* is the comparative form used with a noun, for example, *it's more work, it takes more time*)
4. quicker, slower
5. more touristy

Ask the class for examples of places that they think of as *touristy*, and what makes them *touristy*. Check that students understand this adjective is generally negative in meaning.

Your students might ask about the expression *have a laugh with her* (if you *have a laugh with someone*, you have fun with them) or Lake Como (it is in northern Italy and is a popular tourist destination famous for its scenery). Follow up by asking the class for other words that would fit in the five dialogues, for example in number 2, *Lovely, it's much cleaner/more comfortable than their old one*. Finally, elicit from the class how to decide which form (*more* or *-er*) to use and then refer them to the **Grammar commentary, G3 Comparatives** on page 159.

3 | Pronunciation: the schwa sound

Demonstrate the schwa sound and then say the example sentence yourself. Ask the class if they heard where you made the sound. Typically, the schwa sound is used for the reduced form of the following underlined vowels in fluent speech: *bett<u>er</u>, th<u>a</u>n, t<u>o</u>*. Being able to use the schwa like this helps the fluency and rhythm of spoken English. Tell the students that it will help them say groups of words together without pausing because it takes less time and energy to make the schwa than if the vowel were clearer. To illustrate this, ask them to say *than* with the schwa and then with the clearer vowel, noticing which one required more movement of the mouth. Have the class say the sentences in pairs and then play the recording. Replay the recording sentence by sentence with the class repeating. Follow up with the personalisation questions about what *it* refers to by first modelling some answers yourself.

4 | Speaking

Give the class some guidance by asking them which expressions might be useful in answering the first question and writing them on the board. For example: *It's a bit smaller than the one I had before. It's in a quieter location. The rent's not as high.*

It's important to give the class time to prepare not only *what* they want to say but *how* they want to say it.

Using vocabulary

1 | Phrasal verbs with *up*

You can suggest that students have one page in their notebooks devoted to recording phrasal verbs that use *up*. Ask them if they can remember any others from the unit (e.g. *lock up*).

Answers

I. get 2. pick 3. Cheer 4. look 5. fill 6. mix

Here are some other expressions you might want to draw your students' attention to:

tickets go on sale

have a bite to eat

It's not the end of the world. (This is a fixed expression meaning that the consequences of something are not as serious as they first seem.)

2 Speaking

This exercise gives students an opportunity to use some of the language they have met in this unit while discussing the questions in groups. (Some things that you could *look up* are *a word in a dictionary, a number in a phone book, a price in a catalogue*.)

3 Talking about disasters

The focus here is on language to describe disasters. Keep in mind that some students may have experience with disasters and bereavement. A cautious approach to the discussion is recommended. Ask the class what is happening or has happened in each photo before they do the task. Draw their attention to the language in the expressions and ask further questions:

What are other situations in which people are evacuated?

What does 'totally turned upside down' mean?

What does 'right on the edge' mean?

Apart from fire, what else can spread? (e.g. *disease*)

Where will the house 'go at any moment'?

In many cases more than one answer is possible.

Answers

I. A, B or C. 2. A, B or C. 3. C 4. C 5. A, B (or, by a miracle, C) 6. A 7. B 8. B 9. A 10. B or C 11. B or C 12. B 13. C

4 Speaking

Give a personal example first if you have one or make one up. Before working on this task, brainstorm types of natural disasters and write them on the board. For example:

typhoon, hurricane, earthquake, volcanic eruption, mudslide, avalanche, flooding, tidal wave, forest fire, ice storm

5 Giving bad news

The focus of this task is on language that introduces bad news. Point out that we often use these kinds of expressions because it would seem too abrupt to give the bad news straight away. Draw attention to the expressions used in response to bad news (*Oh, that's awful. Oh, I am sorry to hear that*).

There are two ways of doing the matching task. Students can make dialogues by matching up the questions and answers first, and then check their answers by listening to the recording. Alternatively, they can cover the answers a–h and read 1–8 only. They then listen to the recorded dialogues. After that, they look at the responses a–h and match them up. Finally, they listen again to confirm their answers. This has the advantage of students listening to the same thing twice. If you want students to read the dialogues in pairs, it is easier if you use the tapescript on page 148.

Your students might ask about *passed away*, which is a more indirect way of saying someone has died. Ask them about different expressions they have in their own language. Refer them to the **Real English** note on *have it put down*.

Answers

I. e. 2. c. 3. f. 4. a. 5. h. 6. g. 7. b. 8. d.

The expressions used to introduce bad news are:

a. I'm afraid not.

b. Well, actually, …

c. I don't know how to put this, but …

d. Unfortunately, I'm afraid …

e. I'm sorry, I'm afraid I can't.

f. Well, actually, …

g. Well, actually, …

h. Well, yes, I'm afraid …

6 Role play

Act out the example, and then give the students a few minutes to prepare before they try both the conversations. Ask them to repeat the conversations once or even twice more. Explain that repeating exactly the same thing improves their performance. You might want to give them the homework task of trying to memorise the words and expressions so they can use them to repeat the task again in the next lesson.

Follow-up

This unit has several examples of expressions with the 'delexalised' verbs *get* and *take*. For homework, ask students to go back through the unit and find as many examples as they can for each verb. Tell them to record them on separate pages in their notebooks.

Unit overview

General topic
Talking about the things that interest you.

Dialogue
Dan and Helena have just started going out together and are trying to decide how to spend an evening.

Reading
Some people collect designer carrier bags!

Language input

- Time expressions: *once or twice a month, hardly ever, not as often as I used to,* etc.
- Questions with *how: How much did it cost? How difficult is it?* etc.
- Agreeing: *So do I, Neither do I, Me too,* etc.
- Auxiliary verbs: *do, am, can,* etc.
- Softening with *really: It's not really my thing.*
- Used to: *I used to collect cans when I was younger.*
- Idioms to talk about interests: *It's not really my cup of tea,* etc.
- Expressions with *thing: It's just one thing after another, for one thing, the thing is,* etc.

Language strip

The expressions here are all related to talking about interests. Ask students to look through the strip, identifying any they can see themselves using, both questions (*What sort of music are you into?*) and answers (*I'm a total shopaholic*). You can also tell them to find expressions which use *sort of* or *kind of*. Encourage them to discuss how they would say those expressions in their own language. Point out that they will see some of the expressions used in the unit. You may be asked to explain some of the more idiomatic expressions.

- If you say *I really get a kick out of it* or *I'm really into board games,* you are talking about things that give you pleasure.
- If you say *You can't beat a live gig,* it means that you think there is nothing better than a live musical performance.
- if you're *a shopaholic,* you love to shop. (Compare this with *alcoholic, workaholic* in Unit 1, and *chocoholic.*)

Lead in

Lead in to the unit by asking what students like to do with their free time, and if they had more free time what they would like to do.

Using vocabulary

1 Free time

First talk about how often you do the activities. Encourage the class to ask you questions and then to recall any useful expressions they heard you use. Check that they know *junk shop* (refer them to the photo), and *t'ai chi* (a Chinese martial art practised for health and relaxation). The students can then talk about their answers in pairs. They may find that *often, sometimes* and *never* do not express accurately enough how often they do these things, so give them some more adverbs and expressions (e.g. *rarely, all the time*) as they ask for them. They will meet more expressions on page 21. When they have finished, ask whether any pairs *have a lot in common, don't have much in common, share similar interests.* Ask further questions yourself. For example:
So, what are some good clubs in the area?
What kind of music do they play?

Refer students to the **Real English** note on *junk*. Ask if they have come across any expressions using this word (e.g. *junkyard, junk food*).

Photo opportunity

Ask the class what each photo shows. To work on vocabulary, ask them to think of as many *verb + noun collocations* as they can for each situation. Whichever pair has the greatest number of acceptable collocations wins. Give students an example for each picture to get them started (club – *get a drink,* junk shop – *pick up a bargain,* gym – *lift weights*). Alternatively, ask students to act or write out a conversation which could happen in one of these places, perhaps between two people in the club, or a person joining the gym and an instructor, or between a shopper and a shop owner in the junk shop.

2 Not as often as I used to

Use the photo to introduce the task. Ask questions like:
How old do you think she looks?
How many hours a week does a typical bus driver work?
Do you think she has much free time?

Have the students listen to the recording and complete the answers. Make sure they have a chance to practise saying them. (If your students ask about *fortnight,* tell them it is short for *fourteen nights,* in other words, two weeks.)

Answers

1. often 2. time 3. often 4. every 5. Whenever
6. couple 7. ever 8. used

Photo opportunity

You might want to ask students if it is common to have women bus drivers where they come from. If not, why not? What about women lorry drivers or women pilots? Alternatively, ask students to talk about any bus journeys they regularly make, how they feel about travelling by bus, if they ever chat to people on buses, anything strange or funny or unusual that's ever happened to them on a bus, how they'd feel about actually being a bus driver, etc.

3 How often do you ...?

Have individual students ask you the questions first. Try to use the expressions from **2 Not as often as I used to**. Point out that in spoken English we typically use these kinds of short answers rather than fully formed sentences. As an example, ask them whether *all the time* or *I always get up early on Saturdays* sounds more natural as an answer to question two. Try to add more information in your answers and encourage students to do so too. For example:

A: *So, how often do you have your hair cut?*
B: *Oh, every month or so. It depends. I have it cut more in the summer, but I like my hair longer in the winter.*

A variation on this task is to ask students to first write down how they think their partner will answer each question, and then to check by asking.

4 *How-* questions

Lead in to the task by brainstorming different kinds of questions beginning with *how*. Write them on the board. Students sometimes have problems forming *how-* questions, so this will give you an idea of their needs. Give them the task to complete and again draw their attention to the fact that these questions are typically answered in short phrases. Suggest that they record several examples in their notebooks, possibly on a page entitled *How*.

Answers

1. long 2. far 3. long ago 4. much 5. long 6. well
7. hard/difficult/easy 8. often 9. many 10. worried

For the second task, get students to complete the questions after eliciting some examples with the class as a whole. For example:
How much do you smoke?
How much did you pay for that haircut?

You could either get the students to ask and answer these questions in pairs or to move around asking a different person each question. Remind them to give further details in their answers when appropriate. You could extend this activity by choosing three or four students to take the roles of famous people and then divide the class into small groups to work on interview questions starting with *how*. You can then have a mock press conference with the four celebrities sitting at the front and the rest of the class firing questions at them.

Listening

1 Speaking

Use all or some of these questions for a small group discussion. Give students time to think about what they want to say and how they want to say it. Draw their attention to the collocation *share interests,* and ask for other abstract nouns that collocate with *share* (e.g. *an opinion, ideas*).

2 Before you listen (So what shall we do tonight?)

Explain the situation. You could use the photo at the bottom of the page to generate some discussion and review some of the expressions from the previous units. For example, ask questions like:
How old do you think they are?
How well do you think they get along?
What kind of person do you think he/she is?

Point out that if Dan and Helena *are going out together*, it means that they are boyfriend and girlfriend. People often ask couples the question:
So, how long have you been going out together?

Go through the three statements before students listen to the recording, and make sure that they cover the text. Then check which statement is the most accurate.

Answers

They have less in common than they think.

Let students read the conversation as you play the recording again. Then ask them to fill in the first two or three gaps in pairs, from memory. Play the recording again with pauses so that they can check and fill in the missing words. Do this two or three gaps at a time. Play the recording through one more time, while students follow the text. Listening to the same language again and again is vital for students who want to improve their spoken English. Use the tapescript on page 149 if you want students to read the conversation, or parts of it, in pairs and to see the missing words in blue.

You might want to discuss, or your students might ask you about, some of the expressions in the conversation.

- *So, what do you feel like doing tonight?* is a typical way to start a conversation about your plans for the evening.

- If you *are into something*, you really like it. For example: *I'm really into early jazz at the moment.*

- *You're kidding* is used in response to something someone says that is surprising or unbelievable.

- If *something gets to you*, it means that it tires you out or annoys you. For example: *All this rain really gets to me!*

- *First thing in the morning* means *early in the morning*. Point out that this is relative to when you get up.

- If *something is off the menu*, it means that it is no longer an option.

- If you *give something a go*, you're willing to try it.

If you want to, you could ask students to read through the tapescript and underline examples of vague language (*I don't know, things like that, that kind of thing, I suppose we could, somewhere like*). Encourage them to record any expressions they like in their notebooks.

Refer the class to the **Real English** note on *the thing was*. For practice, give them a couple of conversations to complete:

A: *Have you got that money I lent you?*
B: *Well, the thing is …*

A: *So, are you ready for a great night out?*
B: *Well, the thing is …*

3 | Speaking

Follow up the intensive listening with these group discussion questions.

Using grammar

1 | Agreeing

Some students have problems with these kinds of structures, especially when responding to grammatically negative statements. Give them plenty of practice responding. Go through the examples, pointing out that *Me too* and *Me neither* can be used in response to a question with any auxiliary verb.

2 | Grammar in context

Remind students that in this exercise, two of the responses are correct and they should choose the one that is wrong. These kinds of exercises are a useful alternative to the traditional multiple-choice style questions, where students are exposed to only one appropriate answer.

> **Answers**
>
> The incorrect responses are:
> 1. So have I. 2. Me too. 3. Neither do I. 4. Neither have I. 5. So do I. 6. Me neither.

Before doing the next task, check that the class understands which auxiliaries are used, perhaps by putting a table on the board. For example:
love – do
don't like – do
can't – can
would – would

3 | Auxiliary verb practice

This exercise can be done orally in pairs. Follow up by going through the **Grammar commentary, G4 Using auxiliaries** on page 160.

> **Answers**
>
> 1. So do I. 2. Neither do I. 3. So am I. 4. So have I.
> 5. Neither do I. 6. So would I. 7. So was I.
> 8. Neither can I.

Real English: *What kind of films are you into?*

Exploit this note by first talking about some things that you're really into. Alternatively, you could ask the class to guess what things you're into! Get students to talk with a partner, reminding them to ask for and give further details.

Using vocabulary

1 Not really keen

This activity follows on naturally from the previous activity. Write a statement on the board: *I really love classical music and opera (or spicy food/football)*. Ask the class to agree (*So do I/Me too*). Now ask them how they would respond if they didn't like it. Respond to their ideas and then show them the example conversation. Point out the way we soften the disagreement. Let them hear how the responses sound without *really*. After students have made short dialogues by matching the statements to the responses, play the recording while they follow the tapescript on page 149. Then get students to read the dialogues in pairs.

Answers

1. b. 2. f. 3. a. 4. e. 5. d. 6. c.

The examples of *really* in this exercise are:
a. It's not really my kind of thing/I don't really understand.
b. Really? I'm not really very keen on them myself.
c. It's not really my kind of thing.
d. I don't really like things like that myself.
e. I'm not really that keen on …
f. It's not really my kind of thing.

The final task provides a good opportunity to remind the class that the Coursebook is a rich learning resource. Encourage students to notice, ask about, underline and record interesting collocations and expressions. Give them some examples of questions that they could ask you about language they meet:
What are some other collocations of … ?
What does this expression mean?
Is this a common expression in spoken English?

As you go through the answers, give definitions, other examples, or ask questions to make sure students understand the meanings. Here are some examples:

• If something *is not my kind of thing*, it means that I don't really like it; it's not what I'm into.

• If something *put you off for life*, it means that you had such a bad experience, you never want to do it again. For example: *I had a friend who worked in an abattoir once. It put her off meat for life.*

• If you *don't see the point of something*, it means that you think it's useless or don't know its purpose. For example: *I don't see the point telling you this if you're not listening*! Ask about some things students don't see the point of.

Answers

1. winter sports
2. have fun
3. interested in politics
4. It's not my kind of thing.
5. get hurt
6. classical music
7. I don't see the point of it.
8. It put me off for life.

---

2 I really love it

In pairs, get students to practise talking about what activities they like/don't like doing. Refer to the words in the box. Encourage students to use the language from the two previous activities. For example:
A: *I'm not really very keen on golf myself.*
B: *No, me neither. It looks really boring, doesn't it?*

Make sure students know what *-ing* form of the verb to use with these activities: *I like … playing golf/tennis/football, going snorkelling/windsurfing/surfing/cycling* (if it's just as a hobby), *cycling* (if it's more serious and competitive) and *diving*. Depending on the interests of your students, you may want to extend the vocabulary work on one or two of these sports, with some exercises from the Workbook.

Reading

1 Interests

The focus of this section is *used to*. Let the students hear how this is pronounced, /juːs tə/, and get them to practise it. Students may have come across this structure before, but check that they understand the meaning by asking a few questions. For example:
Is he still into toy trains?

Also point out the surrounding language: *… but don't any more, … when I was younger.*

If students want to record examples, encourage them to include these phrases too. If anyone asks about *'d* in *I'd find* in the first example, this is the contracted form of *I would find*. This use of *would* has a similar meaning to *used to* when it refers to repeated actions (*I'd play with it for hours every day*). Point out the expression *grow out of*. Ask for or give examples of other things you can *grow out of* (e.g. *clothes, sucking my thumb*). Students often ask *What is/are your hobby/hobbies?* so draw their attention to the more typical alternatives.

2 While you read (Are you a bag person?)

Ask if anyone can guess what the title of the article (**Are you a bag person?**) refers to. You could tell students that homeless women who live out of plastic bags are sometimes called *bag ladies*. Tell them they're going to read a text about a rather strange kind of interest – collecting carrier bags! This text is mainly for stimulating light-hearted discussion, so encourage students not to worry about any new words, but if they insist, remember to focus on whole chunks (*just ask straight out for a bag, remain in perfect condition*) or collocations (*hold/take part in an exhibition, tremendous success*), not individual words. Students may ask about several expressions or references:

- If *you wouldn't part with something for the world*, it means that you really want to keep it. For example: *I used to really love this old teddy bear when I was a kid. I wouldn't part with it for the world. In fact, I still have it.*

- *Tesco* is a British supermarket chain, *Marks and Spencer* is a department store, *Harrods* is an upmarket department store, *Gucci*, *Armani*, and *Louis Vuitton* are fashion houses.

3 Speaking

Talk about yourself first. For example:
I have this really cool carrier bag with a map of the London tube on it. When I get bored, I sit down and plan as many ways as I can to get from one place to another.

You can extend the discussion on designer clothes with the photo opportunity below.

Photo opportunity

The picture on page 24 can be used to get a discussion going about brand name products. Ask students to make a list of what they think are the six most famous brands in their country and then to compare their lists with a partner. In pairs, they should then agree on a new top ten. In groups of four, students then discuss how each brand is different, what kind of image it projects, what defines the brand, how it advertises its products, and so on. You could bring in advertisements and ask students to analyse what techniques the companies are using to try and sell their brands. Students could also discuss their own feelings towards brand name products.

Using vocabulary

1 Idioms focus

Here students meet several idiomatic expressions for talking about interests. They might have some difficulty completing the first task if they have never come across the idioms before. One way to help them, before they even look at this page, is to talk about your own interests and try to include some of the idioms. For example:
A lot of my family go hiking on the weekend, but it's not really my cup of tea. Sitting down in front of the telly and watching the football is more up my street. Do you like football? Who do you support? Really, well there's no accounting for taste.

Then introduce the task and ask if students can recall any of the expressions you used.

While checking the answers, say the idioms several times. Tell students to record those that they like in their notebooks or on note cards. Remind them to translate the idioms into their own language.

> **Answers**
>
> 1. cup 2. street 3. own 4. taste 5. accounting
>
> a. There's no accounting for taste. Oh well, each to their own.
>
> b. It's not really my cup of tea.
>
> c. It should be right up your street.
>
> d. It's an acquired taste.

2 Speaking

You could either do this task with students in small groups, or with students moving around the classroom talking about each question. Talk about yourself, either beforehand or afterwards. Alternatively, have the class guess what your answers would be.

3 | Expressions with *thing*

Ask students if they can recall any expressions with *thing* from the dialogue (**So what shall we do tonight?**) on page 22. For example:
the thing is
first thing in the morning
things like that

Get them to do the task and then check their understanding by asking questions for each one:
Why has it been a dreadful day?
What do you think he does when he needs an oil change?
How would she have reacted if she had been really upset?
How would an Indonesian react if you did this?
Can you remember other ways of introducing bad news or a problem? (e.g. *Well, actually, … , Unfortunately, …*)

If someone said about a restaurant *for one thing, it's expensive,* would you expect that there are other things wrong with it?

Answers

1. one thing after another
2. I don't know the first thing about
3. it's just one of those things
4. It's just not the done thing
5. the thing is
6. for one thing

---

4 | Speaking

Use the questions to give the students practice hearing and using the *thing* expressions. Even in monolingual groups, there can be a variety of opinions. You might want do the last question separately. Give an example yourself first:
I don't know the first thing about upgrading computers and I want to get more memory. Can anyone tell me how to do it?

Tell each student to think of three things they want to do but don't know how to. They then move around the class trying to find someone who can help them. Remind them how to agree to negative statements:
A: I don't know the first thing about cooking.
B: Neither do I. Why don't you ask George?

Photo opportunity

The pictures on page 25 can be used to get a discussion going about music. Ask students what bands they're into. Ask students if they play a musical instrument. Would they ever consider joining a band? What kind of music would they play? What are some of the top bands in their country?

Unit overview

General topic

The subject is still interests and free-time activities, but this unit considers women doing sports traditionally done only by men as well as popular leisure activities which can be very dangerous.

Reading

Despite gains in equal rights for women, some areas of British society, such as sport, still have a way to go.

Language input

- *-ing* forms: *I spend a lot of time windsurfing, Mountaineering can be pretty dangerous,* etc.

- Expressions with *all right*: *Are you feeling all right now?* etc.

- Checking you understand: *What? Do you mean just listening to it or actually playing it?*

- Expressions with *would* and *'d*: *I would if I could, that'd be great,* etc.

Language strip

Draw students' attention to the language strip. Ask them to choose a few expressions they find interesting and, on their own, find out more about them. In a later class, they can share what they know as well as work on either of the following ideas. Ask students to choose four questions or four statements and then to discuss what might be said to prompt those expressions. For example, you might say *Won't you end up getting hurt?* if someone says that they are going skydiving. Alternatively, ask students to look at the pictures on page 30 and in groups decide which expressions could be applied to which picture. For example, rock-climbing might prompt *But isn't it dangerous?* Students might need help with the following expressions:

- If something *is a bit off the wall*, it means that it is a little strange. For example: *Don't you think synchronised swimming is a bit off the wall?*

- If something *gives you a buzz*, it means that you find it exciting and that it makes you feel wonderful for a short period of time. For example: *Driving a race car can give you a buzz.*

- You might use the phrase *You wouldn't catch me up in one of those* while talking about hot-air ballooning.

Ask students if they remember meeting *get a kick out of something* and *not my/everybody's cup of tea* in the previous unit. Remind students to add some of the expressions that they want to use themselves to their notebooks.

Lead in

Ask the class to tell you about any unusual interests they have, or tell them about something you are interested in. Have them listen and ask questions. Ask them to recall any interesting expressions or collocations that they heard. Write these on the board.

Using grammar

1 The *-ing* form as a verb

If you haven't already done so, you may want to discuss as a class the **Learning rules and noticing examples** section on page 158 of the **Grammar introduction** before starting this exercise. In some traditional grammars, the terms *gerund* and *participle* may be used to describe *-ing* forms used as nouns and as adverbs/adjectives respectively. Rather than spend a lot of time discussing the finer grammatical details, encourage students to notice and record *-ing* forms as they occur in phrases.

Ask the class to discuss in pairs which of the activities they enjoy doing. Give them some useful expressions like *I've never done that before, I'm not that keen on it, I'm really into it* before they do the task. Point out that there are some useful verb + noun collocations in the list (e.g. *plan holidays, raise money, surf the net*). After they have completed the eight sentences, go over the two patterns. Ask them to sort the time expressions into the appropriate pattern. You might suggest that students record examples in their notebooks in the following ways with personalised examples:

I go	*swimming*	*whenever I can.*
	clubbing	*every weekend.*
I spend	*most of my weekend*	*working in the garden.*
	all my time	*thinking of you.*

Answers

1. surfing the net
2. studying English/Spanish/Russian, etc.
3. raising money for sick animals
4. singing
5. gardening/visiting gardens
6. planning my summer holidays
7. mountaineering/hill-walking
8. helping homeless people

The time expressions are:
1. his whole life
2. most of the winter
3. a lot of time
4. all his free time
5. all her time
6. ages
7. nearly every weekend
8. every Saturday night

Pattern a: whenever I can, as often as I can, quite often, on Tuesdays
Pattern b: most of my evenings, all my Saturday mornings, all my life, half my life

Model some possibilities for the personalised sentences before the students do the task themselves. For example:
I go camping quite a lot in the summer.
I sometimes feel like I spend half my life marking homework.

Encourage them to ask you questions like: *So, where do you go?* This sets an example for them to follow.

2 The *-ing* form as a noun

Although the focus here is on grammar, it's fun to let students argue about the ideas they have. Numbers 1, 2, 5, 6 and 8 in particular can cause fairly heated debate in the right class – and much laughter!

Answers

Possible answers:
1. Ballroom dancing 2. mountaineering 3. Sailing
4. Going off travelling 5. Learning Japanese
6. Helping the poor/homeless/elderly
7. Learning to ride a motorbike 8. Visiting gardens

3 All right

All right is used in several useful expressions. Briefly go over the **Real English** note if you want to before getting the class to match the parts of the conversation. Make sure students hear the stress pattern, *all right,* before they read the conversations. If you think students might have trouble recalling the exact phrase in the second task, give them the first few words of the response on the board. Point out that *It'll be all right on the night* is a fixed expression said to reassure someone who is nervous about an upcoming event like a speech.

Answers

1. c.   2. f.   3. b.   4. a.   5. d.   6. g.   7. e.

4 More *-ing* forms in use

Go through the examples a few times, letting the class hear the stress and intonation patterns before they complete the conversations. Have them practise reading first. Then see if they can remember the conversations without the script. Now ask students to write similar three-part dialogues of their own.

Answers

1. What? Do you mean just watching it or do you actually box yourself?
2. What? Do you mean just watching it or do you actually play yourself?
3. What? Do you mean just going to Chinese restaurants or do you actually make it yourself?
4. What? Do you mean just going to galleries or do you actually paint yourself?
5. What? Do you mean youth culture or Beethoven and things like that?

Photo opportunity

You could use the pictures on page 27 to generate some discussion. Here are some question ideas:
Is anyone into folk dancing? Would you ever do it if someone asked you?

Does anyone know some good places to go camping?

What sort of things can be done to deal with the problem of homelessness?

What is the attraction of mountaineering?

Reading

1 Speaking

These questions help lead in to the topic of the reading text. You could either discuss them in small groups or as a class.

2 Before you read

Tell the students about the text they are about to read and go over the vocabulary. Ask further questions to generate connected language:
What other things do you need a licence for? (e.g. *driving, owning a dog*)
How would you counter the argument that smoking should be allowed in public places?
Have you come across other nouns that collocate with 'commit'? (e.g. *acts of terrorism, murder*)
So, is committing suicide a crime, then?

3 While you read (It's a man's world?)

The task here is to find examples of discrimination. Get the class to compare their answers in pairs. It is wise not to come down too heavily on men, since you don't want to alienate the male students in your class.

> **Answers**
>
> Possible answers:
> Women earn 30% less than men. It's difficult for women to get the top jobs in many companies. Women do more than their fair share of the work in the home. Women's boxing isn't officially recognised.

You can talk about the expression *glass ceiling* now or leave it to **5 Comprehension check**. In either case, students might be interested to learn that it is often used when talking about equal rights for women in the workplace. The image the expression creates illustrates the meaning pretty clearly. You could ask if there are equivalents in the students' own languages.

4 Speaking

Use the questions here to continue the discussion. You may wish to add other groups to the list of people who are discriminated against, depending on your situation.

5 Comprehension check

Give students five minutes to work on this on their own. Then ask them to compare answers in pairs before checking with you. You could also do these questions straight after the reading instead.

> **Answers**
>
> 1. They go off in a huff. (If you *go off in a huff*, it means you are annoyed because of something that happened. For example: *I told my boyfriend I was busy this weekend and he stormed off in a huff.*)
> 2. A glass ceiling.
> 3. British Boxing Board of Control. (Ask about other abbreviations, e.g. *asap, DIY.*)
> 4. No, because she was being sarcastic. (You may need to give students a definition and example: If you *say something sarcastically*, you want to give a meaning that is opposite to what the words seem to say. For example, if it's pouring with rain, you could say sarcastically *What nice weather we're having!* Often sarcasm is conveyed by the tone of the voice, so let students hear your example.)

6 Vocabulary check

Make sure students notice the collocations (*commit a violent crime, take a big risk, do research*). Remind them to record them in their notebooks. Ask a few personalised questions here as you're checking their answers. For example:

Have any of you ever been in a boxing ring? How was it? Did you win?

Are you ever sarcastic?

Is your government doing anything that there's a lot of opposition to at the moment?

Do you like taking risks?

> **Answers**
>
> 1. champion 2. ring 3. sarcastically 4. research 5. earn
> 6. opposition 7. taking 8. crime

Using vocabulary

1 Boxing joke

Play the recording once or twice to show where the speaker pauses and uses intonation to tell the joke well. Encourage students to copy the way the speaker tells the joke. You might want to put students into groups of three or four and have them decide who tells it best. Mimicking is a great way for them to improve the rhythm of their spoken English.

2 Violent or dangerous?

Use the photos to ask if anyone has ever gone climbing, snowboarding or canyoning. Even though some of these activities in the list are very obviously violent or dangerous, encourage students to explain why. For example, it could be argued that football is both violent and dangerous – players get into fights every now and then, they lose their tempers, they get their legs broken, and so on. Discussing these views helps extend students' vocabularies and develop their fluency. Pairs or small groups can discuss each sport while you move around the room to help with vocabulary when necessary. Perhaps make a note of language that was lacking as students gave their views and present that language at the end of the discussion. Give examples of good language that was used too.

You might want to model the two structures before students do the task themselves. For example:
You know I'd quite like to go hang-gliding. I bet it feels great to be up there all alone looking down on everything. I wouldn't go scuba-diving, though. I'd be afraid of sharks.

Also discuss which of the sports aren't typically used with *go* (*play football, do boxing/wrestling/kick-boxing*). The two questions at the end provide another opportunity for students to express their opinions.

Photo opportunity

The following are two ideas for further exploiting the pictures on page 30:

- Ask groups to list what equipment is needed for each of the activities in the photos.
- Divide the class into three groups – a rock climbing group, a footballing one and a snowboarding one. Have each group list why they love their sport so much and then ask them to try to persuade the people from the other groups that their chosen sport is the most exciting.

Using grammar

1 *Would* and *'d*

Would is very common in spoken English, but it is often difficult to explain. Many students will associate it with conditional sentences, and indeed it is often used to make a statement more hypothetical. Another common use is to make statements more tentative (*Would you pass me the salt?*). Rather than going into too much detail about the grammar, focus more on the expressions and the contexts in which it is used. Suggest that students devote one or two pages in their notebooks to expressions with *would*. Encourage students to say these expressions several times chorally and individually until they can say them fluently:
I would if I could …
I'd quite like to …
If you'd rather …
I wouldn't if I were you.
That'd be great.

Answers

1. c.   2. e.   3. a.   4. b.   5. d.

Point out the **Real English** note for *Do you want a lift?* Ask if anyone knows what you would say if you were in the US. (*Can I give you a ride?*)

2 Grammar in context

After going through the answers, have students practise the conversations in pairs. You could also ask them to think about what line comes next. For example, in number 1:
A: *I'd quite like to go out for a meal if that's all right with you.*
B: *So, what kind of food did you have in mind?*

Allow students to be as creative as they want. Follow up with small groups talking about what they'd never be caught doing, etc. Get each group to share some of their sentences with the class as a whole. Refer students to the **Grammar commentary, G5 Would** on page 160.

Answers

1. I'd quite like to
2. That'd be great
3. I would if I could
4. If you'd rather
5. that'd be great
6. I would if I could
7. I'd quite like to
8. If you'd rather

3 Reaching decisions

As well as *would* expressions, these three role-play situations provide an opportunity to recycle previous language from both this unit and Unit 3. Here are some examples you can write on the board before students do the task:

So, what shall we do, then?

We could always go …

I suppose we could …

Why don't we just …

To be honest with you, I'm not that keen on …

It's not really my thing.

Once students have discussed what they would do in each of the three situations, you could then ask them in pairs to write out one of the three conversations. This gives you a chance to monitor more closely and to help out with vocabulary, and it gives the students the chance to consolidate the new language. Alternatively, get them to write out one of the conversations first before they actually do the discussion, as a way of preparing for the stress of talking in real time.

Photo opportunity

See if any students know where the picture on page 31 was taken (Brighton, on the south coast of England) and if any of them have ever been there. Students could then discuss what kind of things they like seeing and doing when they go on holiday – how interested they are in going round old buildings, what they like to do in the daytime and at night, etc. If you have a multi-national class, students could also spend five minutes telling someone from a different country what their own hometown has to offer tourists and visitors.

Review: Units 1-4

The exercises here can be used as a quiz. **4 Speaking** and **6 Look back and check: Describing people**, however, are better done as a discussion in pairs.

1 Tenses

Answers

1. I'm looking
2. likes
3. I do
4. She runs
5. I'm working
6. do you have

2 Multiple choice

Answers

1. a.	3. b.	5. b.	7. b.	9. a.
2. a.	4. a.	6. a.	8. a.	10. b.

3 Comparing

Answers

1. ~~more~~
2. ~~rude~~
3. ~~lower~~
4. ~~more~~
5. ~~dirty~~
6. ~~safe~~
7. ~~lower~~
8. ~~more difficult~~
9. ~~less~~
10. ~~drug addicts~~

4 Speaking

Answers will vary.

5 Conversation

Answers

1. f.	3. g.	5. a.	7. d.
2. c.	4. b.	6. e.	

6 Look back and check: Describing people

Answers will vary.

7 Expressions

Answers

1. haven't you heard
2. I would if I could
3. I'm afraid I can't
4. one of those things
5. not really keen
6. Cheer up

8 Collocations

Answers

1. e.	5. a.	9. n.	13. o.
2. h.	6. d.	10. i.	14. k.
3. g.	7. f.	11. p.	15. l.
4. b.	8. c.	12. j.	16. m.

9 Real English

Answers

1. c.	3. d.	5. f.	7. e.
2. a.	4. g.	6. h.	8. b.

10 Idioms

Answers

1. a. 2. c. 3. b. 4. h. 5. f. 6. g. 7. d. 8. e.

11 What can you remember?

Answers will vary.

12 Vocabulary quiz

Answers

1. By passing your driving test.
2. You are ambitious.
3. Yes, but vegans don't.
4. Very rarely.
5. Nowhere – they have stopped working.
6. Untidy.
7. They commit suicide.
8. You want to start a relationship with them.
9. A blonde.
10. In a pub or a bar.
11. Hardly ever.
12. About someone else's life. If you write a book about your own life, it's your autobiography.
13. They commit crimes.
14. Not very well. You tend to disagree.
15. Their ideas are fixed in a negative way.
16. An only child.
17. When you are upset about something or have a problem you need to talk about.
18. Blow the roof off, damage the house, smash it to pieces.
19. In a ring.
20. Not very well.

 Learner advice: The authors speak!

Answers will vary.

5 Big decisions

Unit overview

General topic
Asking and talking about decisions you have made, and jobs.

Dialogue
Phil asks Jason why he decided to become a fireman and move to London.

Language input
- Past perfect continuous for giving explanations: *I'd been thinking about it for a while.*
- Idiomatic expressions for talking about how easy or difficult something is: *It was a piece of cake,* etc.
- Expressions for talking about jobs: *You'd have to work really long hours,* etc.
- Second conditionals: *You'd look better if you wore a suit.*
- Collocations with *decision*: *a wise decision, the right decision,* etc.
- Questions with *how come: How come you left your job, then?* etc.
- Explaining decisions: *I just got fed up with it,* etc.

Language strip

Have students choose expressions they find interesting and, on their own, find out more about them. In a later class, have them divide the expressions into two groups: those that could start a conversation (*I've decided it's time to leave home*), and those that could be a response to a statement (*What on earth made you do that?*). They should then come up with the next line in the conversation for those expressions in the first group and the initial statement in the conversation for those expressions in the second group. Students might need help with the following expressions:

- If *you can't make up your mind*, you can't reach a decision. For example: *I can't make up my mind about what to do for my birthday.*
- A *dead-end job* is a job with no prospects for promotion. It also suggests the job will get repetitive and dull. For example: *I don't want to end up in some dead-end job.*

- *You don't get a second bite at the cherry* means you don't get a second chance if you fail the first time. A football manager might say this to a player before they take a penalty.
- *On earth* is often used in questions to add emphasis. It usually means you think the answer to the question won't be a simple one or that you are surprised. For example: *How on earth are we going to solve this problem?*

Remind students to add some of the expressions that they want to use themselves to their notebooks.

Lead in

Use the questions in the first task.

Using vocabulary

1 Tough decisions

To introduce the topic, ask students to think of an important decision they have made (or have to make). Ask why they made it and how it turned out. Give a few ideas if necessary: changing jobs, choosing a university, buying a car, etc. Tell them about a big decision in your life and how it worked out. Give the students a few minutes to think and make notes. Ask if anyone would like to talk about their decision. Students should not be forced to talk about something they don't want to. Tell the class that the unit they are going to look at will help them talk more fluently about decisions.

For the ranking task, tell students that they should rank the decisions according to how hard they imagine them to be. Allow a few minutes for them do this on their own before they explain their order to a partner. Write a few useful expressions on the board to help. For example:
I think it would take me ages to decide.
That's a really tough decision.
It was easy for me to make that decision.

Finish off by asking for other examples of *tough decisions.*

2 Who did what?

You could use the pictures to review expressions from the first two units of the Coursebook. Ask questions like:
How would you describe his/her hair?
What kind of person does she/he look like?

Before students listen, ask them to predict which of the decisions in the list above the people made. Play the recording so that students can see if their guesses were correct.

After students check their answers, ask them to recall any expressions that helped them. Write three headings, *Moving house, Changing a job, Stopping smoking*, on the board and list the expressions under the appropriate heading as students call them out. You could extend this by asking them to come up with more expressions to add to each category.

> ### Answers
>
> Speaker 1 decided to move house.
> Speaker 2 decided to change her job.
> Speaker 3 decided to stop smoking.
>
> Possible expressions that help students to find the answers above:
>
> Moving house: things lying around all over the place, get everything all boxed up and into the van, we had to make five trips just to shift everything
>
> Changing a job: every day there was hell, once I'd handed in my notice
>
> Stopping smoking: I had my last one, stubbed it out, the craving really started, I found myself absolutely dying for one

3 What a nightmare!

You could ask students first to divide the expressions into those describing a good situation and those describing a bad situation. Then check that students understand the meanings. Here are some definitions and examples if they are having trouble:

- If something is *in total chaos*, it means that it is very disorganised. For example: *It was total chaos when the bus drivers went on strike.*

- If you say that *it was a real weight off your shoulders*, it means that you are relieved that a situation that was worrying you has been resolved or removed. For example: *It was a real weight off my shoulders when the neighbours from hell moved out.*

- If you *can't stand something any more*, you have had enough of it. Ask whether there is anything your students *can't stand any more*.

- If you describe something with *What a nightmare*, you are emphasising that the situation was really bad.

- If you say *After that, it was plain sailing*, it means something became easy after being difficult to begin with. For example: *It's a bit complicated to get to my house, but once you get out of the city and onto the motorway it's plain sailing.*

After students tick off the expressions, ask them to tell you who said them and about what. Play the recording a final time while they follow the tapescript on page 150.

> ### Answers
>
> Speaker 1: It was total chaos. What a nightmare!
> Speaker 2: It was a real weight off my shoulders. I just couldn't stand it any more.
> Speaker 3: I felt really pleased with myself. After that, it was plain sailing.

Using grammar

1 Giving explanations

Identifying when it is appropriate to use the past perfect is a challenge for many students. Here the past perfect continuous is presented in the context of explaining a decision. This is a useful way of showing how the past perfect is often used to give background information leading up to an action in the past.

You might want to lead into this section by focusing on a decision from the opening task of the unit. Ask questions like:
So, what made you decide to do it?
How were you feeling at the time?

Then go through the explanation at the beginning of the exercise, pointing out how the past perfect can be used to give this kind of background information. Ask students to underline the past perfect continuous in the examples and, if necessary, talk about how this tense is formed.

Get the class to complete the six dialogues, and then, by focusing on the time expressions, you can explain that the extended time period these phrases suggest makes the continuous form more appropriate. There are a lot of useful expressions to draw students' attention to in the dialogues. For example: *I needed a place of my own, I took a month off work, I just decided to give it a go, at least for the time being, I decided to splash out, if you don't mind me asking.* Ask questions about some of these phrases to generate further useful language. For example:

Would you use 'splash out' to describe buying a pencil? If not, what are some things you could 'splash out' on?

What is the purpose of adding 'if you don't mind me asking'? Can you think of some more questions that can be made more tentative if you add this phrase?

If students ask, tell them *how come* is an alternative to using *why*. (There is more on this on page 41.)

Answers

1. 'd been reading
2. 'd been thinking, 'd been trying
3. 'd been doing
4. 'd been arguing
5. 'd been living
6. 'd been having

The time expressions are:

1. since Sally told me about her trip
2. for a while/for ages
3. for years
4. for months
5. since I left home
6. for a while

---

2 Grammar pair work

Before doing this exercise, give students the following patterns on the board:
It was really/mainly because ... , so ...
Well, basically, ... , so ...

Tell them that past perfect continuous verb forms are common in the first slot, and past simple ones in the second slot. Give an example for the first pattern:
Well, basically, her mum had been asking us about it for ages, and I'd been thinking about it too, so we just decided to go ahead.

Encourage students to follow this extended pattern in their answers.

Before students talk about a big decision in their life, model the task for them by talking about a big decision you have made. Encourage them to tell several people about their decision. This repetition of the task helps students develop fluency and gets them used to using new vocabulary and grammar. Tell students to record examples of the past perfect continuous in their notebooks. Remind them to also include the surrounding language because this helps them see the context. Refer students to the **Grammar commentary, G6 Past perfect continuous** on page 160.

Real English

Basically is a common way of introducing an explanation. Let the class hear you say the examples before they practise them themselves. Point out that phrases like this, used at the start of an utterance, often give us time to think about what we are going to say next.

Using vocabulary

1 Idioms focus

The idioms here can be divided into those that describe an easy situation and those that describe a difficult one. After students check their answers, ask them to sort the idioms into the appropriate category. Remind students to record those that they like in their notebooks with an appropriate translation.

Answers

1. cake 2. stone 3. nothing 4. depth 5. sailing
6. done

---

2 Talking about jobs

Answers

The jobs in the pictures are:
bouncer, surgeon, fireman, soldier, and police officer.

Have the students identify the jobs in the photos, and then model the next task. For example:
I wouldn't mind being a surgeon. I imagine it would be really interesting.
I could never be a soldier. I just couldn't kill anyone.

You can also point out the different forms of the verb *be* (*-ing* form, infinitive with *to* and base form) that follow *wouldn't mind*, *I'd quite like* and *could never* respectively. Follow up by asking individuals to tell you which jobs they'd quite like to do or which jobs they could never do and why. If you want to extend the work on jobs, you could use the photos to practise *have to*. Write the following ideas (or your own ideas) on the board:
You'd have to be fit to do a job like that.

You'd have to be quite intelligent to do a job like that.

You'd have to study for years and pass an exam to do a job like that.

You'd have to work long hours or shifts if you did a job like that.

You'd have to have good people skills to do a job like that.

Then discuss as a class or in small groups which statements apply to each job. This will also produce the negative: *You don't have to be particularly fit.*

Using grammar

1 Second conditionals

The second conditional is a term often found in traditional grammar textbooks. It refers to the structure used to talk about situations which seem unlikely or hypothetical. Typically, the structure contains a past form of the verb, a form of *would* and the word *if*. There are several common expressions using the second conditional (*I wouldn't do that if I were you, I would if I could, but I can't*). Encourage students to record these whole expressions in their notebooks whenever they come across them.

You can lead into this section by asking what all the expressions in **2 Talking about jobs** on page 38 have in common (*'d* or *wouldn't*). Ask students why a form of *would* is used in this context. Hopefully, they'll remember the hypothetical use of *would* from the previous unit. After students have filled in the gaps with the missing verbs, discuss the point that was being made in the text:
Is it really true that we all use second conditionals too much?
Is wishful thinking a waste of time?
What kind of second conditionals do you often find yourself saying? Why?

> **Answers**
>
> 1. earned 2. had 3. met 4. wasn't/weren't 5. wanted
> 6. didn't exist

For number 4 in the first task and number 3 in the second task, you might want to point out that *wasn't* is the more informal choice and *weren't* the more formal. Both are considered correct by most speakers of English.

> **Answers**
>
> 1. I'm sure Rachel would understand if you explained it to her.
> 2. If we had more time, we could look round the museums.
> 3. The fact is I'd buy one if it wasn't/weren't so expensive.
> 4. I often think that if I didn't have any children, I'd travel round the world.
> 5. I often think that life would be easier if everybody just told the truth.

2 Likely or unlikely?

This exercise will hopefully reinforce the hypothetical and unlikely nature of the second conditional as well as show how grammar is a matter of choice and depends on how the speaker sees the events they are describing. Refer students to the **Grammar commentary, G7 Second conditionals** on page 161.

> **Answers**
>
> 1. met 2. thought 3. live 4. lived

For the second task, remind students that they can finish the sentences any way they like. They don't have to use the ideas in the Coursebook.

> **Answers**
>
> Here are the answers if students use the ideas a–d.
> 1. b.   2. c.   3. d.   4. a.

Using vocabulary

1 Decisions, decisions

Introduce the task by talking about how you came into teaching. Try to use the word *decision* with some common collocations:
It was quite an easy decision.
Looking back on it, I think it was the right decision.

> **Answers**
>
> 1. right 2. immediate 3. wise 4. wrong 5. unpopular
> 6. joint

After going through the answers, ask students to tell you some verb collocations with *decision* (e.g. *make, reach, take*).

2 Speaking

Follow up with these questions in small groups to reinforce some of the language on this page. Again, you may choose to tell the class your own ideas, either beforehand or afterwards.

Listening

1 Before you listen

Give students the task of predicting what the big decision will be. Ask questions about the expressions:

What kind of jobs do you need to pass a physical for?

If I'm stuck in front of something all day, am I pleased about it?

Apart from once-living things, what else can be described as 'dead', and what can 'dead' mean? (e.g. dead batteries – no power, dead places – quiet/boring)

You can also ask students to think about what the title *Forty a day!* refers to.

2 While you listen (Forty a day!)

Explain the situation and play the recording of the conversation. Students should focus on answering the two questions and cover the text. Next, they should discuss their answers in pairs. Then let students read the conversation as you play the recording again. Ask the students to work in pairs and to fill in the first two or three gaps from memory, before you play the recording with pauses so that they can check and fill in the missing words. Do this two or three gaps at a time until the end. Play the recording through one more time with students following the text. You may want students to read the conversation, or parts of it, in pairs using the tapescript on page 150.

Answers

1. Jason decided to give up smoking in order to become a fireman and to move to London.

2. He decided to give up smoking because it was destroying his lungs and he needed to pass the physical to get into the fire brigade. He joined the fire brigade because he wanted to do something exciting and different. He moved to London mostly because of work, but also because he was fed up with where he was living.

Here are some expressions that you might want to explain:

- Refer students to the **Real English** note. *Good for you* means *Well done.* Ask if students know any other expressions that could be used instead.

- *Tell me about it* means *I agree with/understand what you are saying. I've had this problem too.*

- *Just as well* is used to say that what someone did was a good thing. For example: *It was just as well I bought my house five years ago. Prices have almost doubled since.*

- If you *push bits of paper round the desk*, it means that you are doing boring office job tasks.

- If you *are fed up with something*, it means that you are bored or tired of it. Ask students if there is anything they *are fed up with.*

3 Speaking

You can turn this into a more extensive discussion by splitting the class into three groups. One group lists reasons why some people decide to move to big cities; the second group lists reasons why some city dwellers decide to move to the countryside; the third group lists reasons why some people never even consider moving from where they grew up! Then put students in groups of three – one from each group – and ask them to share their ideas. Keep the class in these same groups of three to discuss the questions in the Coursebook.

Using vocabulary

1 How come?

To lead in to this activity, ask students to recall any questions using *how come* from **1 Giving explanations** on page 37. Then ask if they can tell you how the structure of a *how come* question is different from a *why* question (*how come* does not use forms of the auxiliaries *do* and *be*). Let the class hear you say the examples, especially the stress pattern. Get the students to complete the twelve sentences in pairs and then check their answers all together. You could also ask them to ask each other the questions, making up suitable answers before they work on their own questions.

Answers

1. Why did you pay so much for your car?
2. Why did you get here so early?
3. Why did you refuse the invitation?
4. Why didn't you accept the job in LA?
5. Why are you so interested in Tibet?
6. Why isn't there any beer left in the fridge?/Why is there no beer left in the fridge?
7. how come
8. why
9. why
10. how come
11. why
12. how come

2 | Jokes!

Here is another chance for students to practise stress and intonation patterns. After completing the punch lines, they can try saying the jokes along with the recording.

Answers

1. I want to be ready in case there's an accident!
2. I wanted to be near my mum!
3. Because I left the plane tickets on it!
4. They didn't look!

3 | Explaining your decisions

These expressions are quite common, but if students are having trouble, give them the first word for each one. When they are checking their answers, ask them to tell you which expression means *no particular reason (I just felt like it)*. Practise the expressions chorally and individually. It is important that students are able to say them easily and fluently as complete natural expressions. You might want the class to mark the main stresses in each sentence in their Coursebooks.

Answers

(Main stress underlined)
a. We just got <u>bored</u> with each other.
b. I've always been <u>in</u>terested in it.
c. I'd always <u>wanted</u> to.
d. I just got fed <u>up</u> with it.
e. I just <u>felt</u> like it.
f. A friend of mine recom<u>men</u>ded him.

1. I'd always wanted to.
2. A friend of mine recommended him
3. I just got fed up with it.
4. I just felt like it.
5. I've always been interested in it,
6. We just got bored with each other.

After students complete the six dialogues, get them to practise saying them in pairs. To help students with the conversation activity, tell them two or three things about yourself using some of the expressions and recycling any other relevant language from this unit.

6 Flying

Unit overview

General topic
Flying and smoking!

Reading
A woman gets arrested for secretly smoking on a plane.

Language input
- Adjectives, strong comparatives: *It was much better than I thought it would be.*
- Strong adjectives: *Scary? It was terrifying!* etc.
- Vocabulary connected with flying: *your boarding pass, the cabin crew,* etc.
- Expressions with *watch, see, look: Here, look out of the window, Can you see anything wrong?* etc.
- Gerunds and infinitives: *I clearly remember posting your letter, I must remember to post your letter,* etc.
- Smoking vocabulary: *a heavy smoker, put out a cigarette,* etc.
- Expressions used to play for time: *Well, I'd have to think about that,* etc.

Language strip

Have students choose any expressions they find interesting and, on their own, find out more about them. In a later class, ask them to share the information. For a small group activity, you could ask students to find the expressions that might be used by airline staff and crew and expressions which a passenger might say. You might need to explain some of the following expressions:

- If you *have no head for heights*, you don't like being high up. For example: *I'll never fix the gutters on my house – I just have no head for heights.*
- If you don't like smoking, you might not want a partner who does because *it would be like kissing an ashtray.*
- If you say *It's a free country*, you are responding to someone who may be questioning whether what you are doing is allowed. For example: *Why can't I park here? It's a free country!*
- If you *don't have the will power to give up something*, it means that you find it really difficult to stop doing something because you can't resist the temptation. We often use this phrase to talk about giving up smoking.

- *You're more likely to get killed crossing the road* is a fixed expression often used to say that what you are doing is not that dangerous statistically. It is usually said about smoking or flying.
- You would say *Mind your own business* to tell someone rudely that they shouldn't ask or talk about something that is personal.
- *Toilets engaged* means that the toilets are occupied.

Lead in

Before doing the first task in this unit, get the students thinking and talking about the subject of flying. Ask them to brainstorm questions on the topic and write them on the board. Here are some examples to get them started:
Have you ever flown? Who with?
How do you decide which airline to fly with?
What do you think the best airline is? Why?
Do you like airports? Why/why not?

Once you have several questions, students can discuss them in small groups. This is a good way to see what they know already.

Reading

1 Your captain speaking

This first task focuses on rules. You could ask students to work individually first, and then discuss in pairs. Give them some expressions to help them check their answers:
A: *Are you sure about that?*
B: *Yes, definitely, I'm pretty/fairly sure./No, I'm not too sure.*

You might want to point out some collocations in the sentences, for example, *pack luggage, strictly prohibited.*

Answers
1. False, but you must say at check-in who packed your luggage if you didn't do it yourself. 2. False 3. True
4. False 5. True 6. True

Before having the students work on the next task, you could give them some examples of language to talk about rules on the board:

You have to …
… is strictly prohibited.
You can … if you want to.
… are/aren't permitted.
… is not allowed.

Answers

Possible answers:

7. Smoking is not allowed during take-off and landing. In fact, most flights are completely non-smoking these days.

8. You can usually use a CD player, but not during take-off or landing.

9. You have to take off high-heeled shoes in an emergency because they damage the escape chute.

10. Hand luggage should either be kept in the overhead lockers or under the seat in front of you.

11. You can use the toilet at any time except when the seatbelt sign is on, when you have to remain in your seat.

12. Seats have to be in the upright position during take-off and landing.

13. You only need to have your seatbelt on when the seatbelt sign is on.

14. Some airlines have special cots for babies. During take-off and landing the baby usually has to be held.

2 | Before you read

The words in the box all come from the article on page 43, and by discussing them students may be able to predict the story. After students have sorted the words into groups, have them discuss what they think happened in the article. Encourage them to use the words in complete phrases and write some of their predictions on the board.

Answers

(*Nervous* could be in all three categories!)
air travel: touched down, nervous, refuelling, cabin crew, on board
the law: handcuffed, prosecuted, fined, arrested, nervous
smoking: light up, puff, nervous

3 | While you read (The cost of a cigarette)

Ask students if they remember the word *craving* from the first listening task in the previous unit. Ask how someone would feel if they were a heavy smoker and had a long non-smoking transatlantic flight. Go through the questions and then let students read the article to see how it compares with their predictions. They can then discuss the three questions in pairs. Encourage the class to answer in their own words.

Answers

1. Because she was so nervous, she felt she just had to have a smoke to calm her down.

2. When the plane finally landed at Heathrow.

3. She was handcuffed. She was prosecuted and then fined £440.

4 | Speaking

The questions here allow students to discuss their reaction to the article and to give their own views on smoking. In many countries the banning of smoking in public places is a hot topic. The questions could be discussed either in small groups or as a class.

5 | Vocabulary check

As always the article is a good source of natural English. Encourage your students to notice, ask about and record in their notebooks interesting expressions and collocations. While they are completing the task here, remind them that they are not just focusing on the individual word but also the surrounding language. Give paragraph references if you want to save time. *Legal aid* refers to the financial assistance (usually from the state) that is provided to people without enough money to pay legal fees.

Answers

1. handled (the pressure) (paragraph 2)
2. avoided (flying) (paragraph 2)
3. touched (down) (paragraph 3)
4. (no) sign (of her) (paragraph 3)
5. relations (between) (paragraph 4)
6. turned (really cold) (paragraph 4)
7. expecting (some important mail) (paragraph 5)
8. (make a) fuss (paragraph 5)
9. legal (aid) (paragraph 5)
10. (second-class) citizens (paragraph 5)

Ask students further questions when checking their answers to produce connected language. For example:
How well do you handle pressure?

What countries does your country have good relations with?

Do you ever avoid complaining because you don't want to make a fuss?

Using vocabulary

1 Flying vocabulary

Here is a further chance for students to work on flying vocabulary. You could follow up this task in a later class by writing each half of several collocations on separate slips of paper – enough for every student – and having students walk around saying their half until they find their partner. This is a great way to review collocations and to get students into pairs. Use the questions to give further practice in small groups. Talk about any personal experiences or those of someone you know.

Answers

1. g.   2. f.   3. b.   4. c.   5. j.   6. a.   7. h.   8. i.
9. d.   10. e.

---

2 Role play

Lead into this task by asking the class about the photo of the billboard. Ask where they think it is situated and who it is aimed at. Ask if they always call home when they reach their destination. Explain the situation of the role play and get the students into pairs. Give them five minutes to prepare what they are going to say. Give them examples of the kinds of questions they could ask you as they prepare. For example:
What verb collocates with 'an unscheduled stopover'?

What expression can I use to say the door of the overhead locker would not open?

You might want to give students the opening lines of the conversation to get them started:
A: *Hi, (Bill).*
B: *Is that you, (Ben)? Where are you calling from?*
A: *I'm in (Amsterdam). We've just landed.*
B: *Glad you made it safely. So, how was the flight?*
A: *It was the flight from hell!*

For homework, students could then write up the conversation, and could even role-play it again at the start of the following lesson with a different partner. Remember that repeating the same task once or twice usually improves students' performance.

3 Watch, see, look

These three verbs can be confusing for students. You could go into the differences of meaning, but it's probably more efficient and useful for them to remember how each is used in various phrases. Tell students to devote one page for each of these verbs in their notebooks and to collect examples as they come across them. Talking about equivalent verbs in their own languages can be very interesting, especially if you have a multilingual class. Again remind students to translate the phrases they record, not just the words. If students don't know what *loo* in number 7 means, ask if they can guess. You could give them some other words for *toilet*, if you are so inclined.

Answers

1. see   2. see, looks   3. watch   4. seen   5. watch
6. look   7. watch   8. see   9. seen   10. looked, see

---

4 Flying joke

Let students read the joke and try to decide on possible endings before you play the recording. Pause the recording before the gapped punch line and ask students to shout out their endings. Then give them the punch line, before getting them to practise telling the whole joke to each other in pairs. (The punch line is in the tapescript on page 150.)

Tell the class a nightmare flying story you know. It doesn't necessarily have to be something that has actually happened to you. It could be a news item, an urban myth or even another flying joke. The Internet is always a great source of such items. Get students to tell each other any stories/jokes that they know. Supply a couple of your own just in case ideas are in short supply.

Using vocabulary

1 Adjectives: strong comparatives

This task practises another way in which comparatives are often used in everyday speech. Before doing the task, ask students to tell you of anything that turned out differently from what they expected (a place they moved to, the course they are currently taking, or this Coursebook!). Then say the examples several times, allowing students to hear the stress patterns. Ask if they can tell you what pattern they notice, and write it on the board for them to transfer to their notebooks:
adjective … *much* + comparative form of a synonymous adjective.
terrible … much worse
good … much nicer

Have pairs practise saying the examples before working on numbers 1–6. While there are no definite answers for this task, some answers are more probable than others. Here are some likely answers, but allow others too if they make sense.

Answers

Possible answers:

1. Oh, it went well – much better than I'd expected.
2. Yeah, it was sweltering – much hotter than I thought it would be.
3. Great – much easier than I'd expected.
4. Oh, it went well – much better than I'd expected.
5. It was fine – much nicer than I thought it would be.
6. Yeah, it was really interesting – much better than I'd expected.

You may want to draw attention to the following collocations: *my move/exam/presentation went well*. Ask for examples of other things that can go well. Depending on how well your class know you, you could get them to ask you questions before working in pairs. For example:
A: *How was my homework?*
B: *It was pretty good, much better than last time.*

2 Strong adjectives

Say the two examples and ask the class to tell you what structural pattern (adjective ... stronger adjective) and intonation pattern (rising on the first adjective) they notice. Have students practise saying the examples before they complete the eight dialogues. (Devon is a mainly rural county in south-western England.)

Answers

1. Hot? It was boiling!
2. Big? It's enormous!
3. Cold? It's freezing!
4. Quiet? It's dead! (Remember Crawley in **Forty a day** in Unit 5.)
5. Surprised? I was shocked!
6. Small? It's tiny!
7. Good-looking? He's gorgeous!
8. Scary? It was terrifying!

Next, work on matching the following lines of the conversation. Have pairs practise reading the conversations by using the tapescript on page 151. After checking the answers, you could elicit more adjective/stronger adjective pairs (*not very nice/disgusting, difficult/impossible, silly/ridiculous*) and then have students use them in pairs to write mini-conversations like those in numbers 1–8. Encourage them to continue the conversation. Here are some expressions you may want to talk about in this section:

- If you say that *there's no way that you'll catch me doing that again,* it means that you will never do it again. For example: *You'll never catch me driving into central London again.*
- If *you can hardly swing a cat* in a place, it means there is not much room.
- If you say that someone *will die when they see someone/something,* it means that they will be very surprised – in a good way.
- In Britain *a solicitor* is someone who gives legal advice and can represent you in court for less serious offences.

Answers

1. e.   2. c.   3. b.   4. f.   5. h.   6. d.   7. g.   8. a.

Using grammar

1 Gerunds and infinitives

This area of grammar often frustrates students because it seems there are no 'rules' to help them decide whether an infinitive or a gerund form follows a certain verb. Although there are some guidelines – a gerund will follow a preposition – tell students that a good way to learn is to focus on whole expressions. For example:
Please try to call when you get a chance.
Why don't you try dialling 001 before the number?

Go through the examples, asking what two patterns the students notice. Ask if they can explain the difference in meaning between the two example sentences with *remember.* One explanation is *remember* + gerund usually refers back from the time of speaking, and *remember* + infinitive usually refers forward. Give students several examples to make this clear:

I can still remember feeling nervous before my first day at school.

I must remember to call my mum tomorrow.

You can also give students typical sentence starters:
I must remember to ...
Please remember to ...
Did you remember to ...
Do you remember ... -ing?
I clearly remember seeing ...
I still remember ... -ing

Ask students to complete these sentences in ways that are true for them and put them in their notebooks.

Go through the **Grammar commentary, G8 Gerund and infinitive** on page 161 before trying the task, as it explains other verbs such as *forget* and *try* with typical examples. You should also point out that when we talk talking about general tastes, *love* and *prefer* are followed by gerunds:

I really love being able to have a lie-in on Sundays.

My husband likes being around the house but I prefer getting out in the fresh air.

However, to talk about tastes and preferences on specific occasions, we usually add *would* to the verb, and then use an infinitive to follow:

I'd love to go to Greece again this summer.

We could go out tonight, if you want, but personally, I'd just prefer to stay in.

Begin and *start* can be followed by either gerund or infinitive without any change in meaning, although *begin* is more generally followed by an infinitive, and *start* is more generally followed by a gerund. As you check the answers, give a typical sentence for each. For example: *I'll ask him to do it when I see him.*

> **Answers**
>
> 1. G/I 2. I 3. I 4. G 5. G/I 6. I 7. G/I 8. G/I
> 9. G 10. G 11. G/I 12. G/I 13. G 14. I 15. G/I
> 16. I

2 Practice

Complete a couple of these sentences yourself. For example:

I'll never forget walking into my first class.

I must remember to pay the bills.

Then encourage the class to ask you further questions. The personalised sentences that students write will help them learn the 'rules'. Tell students to talk about what they wrote with a partner.

3 Grammar check

This exercise gives further practice. You could have students check the answers in pairs with one person reading the sentence like this:

Why did you decide BLANK English?

The other person, without looking at the Coursebook, repeats the sentence with the missing verb form:

Why did you decide to learn English?

> **Answers**
>
> 1. to learn 2. to go 3. in travelling 4. with working
> 5. with doing 6. to get 7. to go

4 Grammar in context

This exercise reviews the forms presented in **3 Grammar check** within the context of talking about decisions. One fun way to start this exercise is to put students in pairs and ask them first to think of the *most predictable* answers that people might give to the first question. For example:

I wanted to do something different.

I was fed up with doing the same thing, day in, day out.

Write these answers on the board, helping with vocabulary where necessary. Then ask students to think of *the funniest* or *strangest* answers they can to the question. For example:

I wanted to become a crocodile trainer.

I decided to retire at twenty-two.

They can then answer the other questions as they wish.

> **Answers**
>
> Possible answers:
>
> 1. I wanted to do something different for a change. I was fed up with doing the same old thing, day in, day out.
>
> 2. I was bored with Bournemouth! I was interested in the fashion industry, and thought it would be a good place to study it.
>
> 3. I wanted a bit more freedom than he/she was giving me. I didn't want to settle down just yet.
>
> 4. I was trying to save money. I was just fed up with people saying that I smelled like an ashtray!

Using vocabulary

1 Smoking

Before doing this exercise, ask students to recall any expressions in the language strip that are connected with smoking. For example:

Passive smoking

Who wants to kiss an ashtray?

Encourage students to write any collocations that they didn't know in their notebooks.

> **Answers**
>
> a. smoker b. cigarette c. cigarettes d. cigarette
> e. smoking
>
> 1. heavy, occasional 2. give up, started 3. put out
> 4. ends 5. advertising 6. smoking

2 Speaking

Have small groups of students discuss the questions here. You could bring in some examples of cigarette advertising from magazines for them to look at. This would be a good exercise to do just before you have a break!

3 Playing for time

Lead in to this exercise by asking some quick-fire questions to individual students. For example:

Why are you wearing blue today?

Why do you think Mondays always seem longer than Fridays?

You can then explain how 'delayers' help us with difficult questions by giving us time to think. Play the recording and let students practise saying the examples. Make sure students sound hesitant and follow the intonation patterns! For questions 1–5, students are not expected to have real answers, although obviously some may. The important point is to practise using the expressions confidently.

4 Role play

This gives students a chance to recycle a lot of the language presented in this and the previous unit in a fun context. First, as a class, decide the name of the famous person to interview and give students time to prepare their questions in pairs. Only then select someone to pretend to be this famous person. This keeps the whole class as involved in the task as possible. A homework task that can follow on from this is to write an imaginary interview with a different celebrity – each student choosing someone they like and know about – trying to use as much of the language from this unit as possible.

Photo opportunity

The photo of Prince William could be used to extend the conversation started during **4 Role play**. Ask students:

What is it like to be famous?

Would you like to be famous?

What would you like to be famous for?

Why wouldn't you want to be a celebrity?

Unit overview

General topic
Talking about plans and intentions for the weekend.

Dialogue
Steve and Ken discuss their plans for the coming weekend.

Language input
- Planning expressions: *I guess I'll probably ... , I'm going to try to ...* , etc.
- The future with *'ll, going to*, present continuous, and present simple: *I'll only be a minute, We're going to catch the early train, I'm leaving at the end of the month, The last bus leaves at 11:15.*
- Other expressions to talk about the future: *I've got somebody coming round, I'm supposed to be doing something*, etc.
- Pronunciation of *'ll*
- Collocations with go: *I'm going on a date, I'm going out to see a film*, etc.
- Vocabulary: *meeting, appointment, date*
- Idioms: *You must be joking! Long time no see!* etc.

Language strip

Have students choose any expressions they find interesting and, on their own, find out more about them. In a later class, ask them to share the information. For a small group activity, ask them to find expressions using the present continuous (e.g. *Doing anything this weekend?*) and expressions most likely said on a Friday (*Have a good weekend*). Students could also underline the expressions they could see using about themselves (*I think I'll just laze about*). Alternatively, they could find all the questions and write a response to each one. You might need to explain some of the following expressions:

- If you *laze about*, you relax and don't really do much. For example: *On Sundays all I want to do is just laze about.*
- You say *I just live for the weekend* to show that for you the weekend is the most important and enjoyable time of the week.
- If you *pop over to a place*, you go there for a short time. For example: *I'm just popping over the road for a sandwich.*

- If you *crash out at someone's place*, you sleep there, usually on the floor or the sofa. For example: *Don't worry about driving home; you can crash at my place.*
- A *car boot sale* is an event, usually at the weekend, where lots of people sell things they don't want out of the back of their cars.
- If you *have some people round*, you invite them to your home for dinner, drinks, games, etc. For example: *I'm sorry I can't go out tonight. We're having some people round.*
- You use the expression *It's not my idea of an exciting weekend* to say that someone's plan for the weekend doesn't sound fun to you. Ask students to give you some examples they could say this phrase about.

Remind students to record the expressions they think would be useful in their notebooks.

Lead in

You can use the photos on page 48 to lead in to the unit. Ask the class about each picture:
- *What is the place shown in the first picture? (a theatre box office) How often do you go to the theatre?*
- *What is happening in the second picture? What's in the buggy? Where's the baby? Do you have to spend ages waiting outside clothes shops for your partner?*
- *Where do you think the women in the third picture are going? Why do they look serious?*

Before moving on to the first exercise, you can ask the class whether they do any of the activities in the pictures at the weekend.

Using vocabulary

1 A typical weekend

Have students tick off the activities they do alone and then compare their answers with a partner. Write some time adverbs (e.g. *most weekends, almost every weekend, every other weekend*) on the board to help students say a bit more about each activity that they actually do: how often they do it, and where. Draw students' attention to some of the verb collocations: *do the shopping, tidy up your flat, do some studying, catch up with your e-mails/work.* You can then talk about the things you spend your weekend doing.

2 | Planning expressions

Point out the **Real English** note on *What are you up to this weekend?* Ask a few students the question *What are you up to this evening/weekend?* Then let them ask you. Try to use some of the expressions 1–8:
I guess I'll probably (do a bit of shopping).
Unfortunately, I've got (a lot of homework to correct).

Set the scene and explain the task. Before playing the recording, say all the phrases so that students know what they sound like. You will probably need to play the recording two or three times. Once students have identified the expressions, you could ask them to use them to reconstruct as much as they can remember about Gavin's plans for the weekend. Then have them read the tapescript on page 151 together and underline the expressions. Ask them what they think a couple of the other expressions here mean:
the place is a tip (the place is untidy)
I've got a big night (I'm doing something exciting)
have a lie-in (stay in bed and get up late)

Finally, give students time to practise saying the eight expressions.

Answers

The expressions Gavin uses are:
1. I guess I'll probably
2. I'm going to try to
3. Unfortunately, I've got to
4. I imagine I'll
5. I guess I'll probably

---

3 | Speaking

Before starting this task, make sure students understand the expressions *a tip, the telly* and *a big night out*. Talk about yourself first so that they can hear these phrases in context.

Using grammar

1 | Four different future forms

Many students believe that *will* is the only future form in English. Although *will* is often used to express the future, other structures are also used. In this exercise, students are shown four ways to talk about the future (the contracted form *'ll, going to,* the present continuous and the present simple). Go through the examples and then have students match the descriptions to the sentences.

Tell them that in deciding which future form to use, they should consider *why* they think the event being described is going to happen: is it scheduled, like a timetable; is it an arrangement that has already been made; is it a sudden, on the spur of the moment decision?

Answers

a. going to
b. present simple
c. present continuous
d. 'll

In checking the answers, ask where students think *I'll have the chicken* is said (a restaurant) and what *India play Australia in the final next month* is about (probably cricket). You may want to point out that *India* here refers to a team and that, since it is a collective noun, it takes the plural form of the verb.

2 | Grammar discussion

This task reinforces the point about how the speaker's relationship to the event determines which future form to use. Have students discuss the questions after the examples in pairs and then check the answers. This is probably a good opportunity to mention that it takes time to master these differences and that they are guidelines rather than strict rules. As always, noticing natural examples and recording them in their notebooks will help.

Answers

1. I decided earlier, before now.
2. It's a scheduled event.
3. I decided now, at the moment of speaking!
4. Yes this is a plan; they know about it already.

---

3 | Grammar check

Once students have done the exercise on their own, ask them to discuss in pairs how they reached their decisions. When going through the answers, draw attention to the fact that the context helps decide which form to choose. For example, in number 4 the present continuous would probably be used as the speaker is discussing arrangements he/she has already made. It's important to stress that the answers given here are *probable*. Remind students that the forms the speaker chooses depend on how he/she perceives the event at the time of speaking. The same event can be perceived in more than one way.

Answers

1. I'll do
2. gets in
3. I'll do
4. I'm going
5. is going to give
6. I'm going to sneeze

Answers

Steve is going out for dinner with his parents tonight to a little French place near his house. He's got to get up early on Saturday to do some cooking and clean the house because he's got some people coming over. They'll probably go and see a film in the evening. Ken is probably just going to stay in tonight because on Saturday night he's going to a party on a boat. On Sunday, he's got to do some things for work.

4 | Grammar in context

This exercise uses the four different future structures to talk about plans for the weekend – the topic of this unit. Have students do the exercise in pairs. Encourage them to record and learn whole sentences from these examples, especially those that they see themselves using. You might want to talk about why someone would have a big night out the day before their brother's wedding. Ask whether they have traditions like *stag* and *hen nights*.

Answers

1. c. 2. a. 3. d. 4. b. 5. h. 6. g. 7. e. 8. f.

The question that follows the exercise gives students the opportunity to use some of the structures and expressions to talk about their plans for next week. Give them five minutes to prepare and then have them move around the class talking to different people. You can join in, too. When you have finished the exercises on this page, refer students to the **Grammar commentary, G9 Talking about the future** on page 161.

Listening

1 | While you listen (Thank goodness it's Friday!)

Ask students if they know the expression TGIF (*Thank goodness/God it's Friday*) and ask them to explain why we might say it. Then read the introduction to set the scene and ask students to listen for the answer to the question. Make sure that they cover the text. Get them to discuss the answer in pairs. Next, let them read the conversation as you play the recording again. Then ask the students to fill in the first two or three gaps from memory in pairs before you play the recording again, this time with pauses so that they can check and fill in the missing words. Do this two or three gaps at a time until the end. Play the recording through one more time with students following the text. Remember that listening to the same language again and again is vital for students who want to improve their spoken English. If you want students to read the conversation, or parts of it, in pairs, use the tapescript on page 151.

There are several expressions that you may want to explain or that your students may ask about:

- If *the week's been dragging*, it means that time seems to be passing slowly and it has been boring and/or difficult. Ask students for other nouns that we can use in this way (*a meeting, a lesson, a film*).
- *Whereabouts* is used in questions to ask precisely where. For example: *Whereabouts in Spain are you from?*
- *A while ago* means an indefinite time in the past. For example: *I saw her a short while ago, in the café over the road.*
- We use the expression *No rest for the wicked* to make fun of friends (or ourselves) when they/we have to work and we/they don't.

If students ask about individual words in the conversation, use the opportunity to extend and develop their vocabularies by giving several collocations and typical phrases containing the word. For example, if someone asks about *docks*, you can explain that it is where ships are loaded and unloaded in a harbour and then give some typical collocations and phrases: *dry dock, down by the docks, dock worker*.

Point out the **Real English** note on *Tell me about it!* and get students to talk about equivalents in their own languages.

2 | Speaking

Use the questions here as a follow-up to the conversation on page 50. You could either discuss them in small groups or as a class. You can also use the photos on pages 50 and 51 to give more speaking practice. Ask if anyone does any of the activities in the pictures on weekends. Ask questions like:
Do any of you ever do parachute jumps or anything like that? Walk along the beach? Go sailing? Go flying? Go for a drive? Wash your car? Go to the market and do the shopping? Work out in the gym? When? How often?

This is a good chance for students to re-use some language from previous units. Encourage the use of the time expressions from page 13 in Unit 1. If anyone in the class does something particularly interesting or strange at the weekend, you could recycle the *How-* questions from page 21, by having the rest of the class ask questions (e.g. *How easy is it to sail a boat?*) to interview the student. The interviewee, in turn, may want to use some of the delayers on page 47 when answering.

Using grammar

1 More ways of talking about the future

In this exercise, students are given some other common ways to talk about the future. Write the four patterns on the board and tell your students to record several examples for each pattern in their notebooks as they are working through the following tasks.

1. *I've got (a person/some people) … -ing*
   This pattern is common with the verbs *arrive*, *visit* and *come* and refers to something already planned.
2. *I've got to/I have to …*
   This is typically used to say that you have an obligation at the time of speaking to do something in the future; it is sometimes something you don't want to do.
3. *I'm supposed to be -ing … but …*
   This pattern is used to describe previous arrangements you have made that you think could be changed.
4. *I might be -ing*
   You use *might* like this to show that you are not sure about what you're going to do.

Play the recording so students can hear the pronunciation and intonation patterns. Then get them to practise saying the examples themselves. You should then go over the explanation of these different forms by referring students to the **Grammar commentary, G10 More ways of talking about the future** on page 162.

Answers

Probable answers:

1. I've got a friend coming round to help me with my homework on Sunday.
2. I'm supposed to be going shopping with a friend on Saturday, but I'll probably stay at home.
3. I might be going to the cinema, but I'm not sure yet.
4. I've got to write an essay this weekend.
5. I've got to clean my flat this weekend.
6. I think Steve might be having a party tomorrow night.
7. I'm supposed to be meeting some friends on Sunday for lunch, but I don't know if I'll feel up to it.
8. I've got my mother coming round on Saturday afternoon.

---

2 Role play

For this role play to really work, you will need to spend a few minutes exploring common ways of inviting people, as in the examples. Usually, the speaker mentions the event – *We're going to have a party next weekend* – and then extends an invitation – *and we'd love you to come along, if you're free.* Draw students' attention to the five-step conversation that occurs and write it on the board:

1. invitation
2. polite refusal + reason
3. asking if these plans could be changed
4. saying they can't
5. closing comment

Have students write a short dialogue in pairs, following this pattern and using the expressions:
Oh, I'd love to, but I'm afraid I can't.
I've already arranged to …
Well, I would if I could, but …

Then practise the dialogue together. Follow up by having students walk around, inviting other people, using the same pattern. Finish by having small groups or the class as a whole discussing whether they would ever turn down an invitation to do any of the activities shown in the photographs at the top of the page.

3 Famous futures

Lead in to the task by asking what kind of music students are into and what favourite songs they have. Then ask them if they can complete the four lines from songs and whether they recognise the songs. You could even ask if anyone could sing them. Students may wonder about the use of *shall* here. *Shall* can be used in a similar way to *will*, although in *We shall overcome* it implies more of an external obligation (for the good of society). After completing 1–4, you could ask the class to go home and try to find some more songs with future forms in them for homework, make a note of them and think about why particular verb forms are used. Start the next class by asking students to share their findings.

Answers

1. shall   2. 'll   3. 'll   4. gonna

Get the class to discuss the quotations in pairs. With some classes, some of the quotations could lead into further discussions. The George Bernard Shaw quote might lead to a debate about who should rule the world:

Who should rule the world? More young people? More women? More people from different kinds of backgrounds?

What difference would it make?

Which leaders are most in touch?

Which are most out of touch?

Similarly, the Voltaire quote could be used to lead into a discussion on the pros and cons of censorship:

Is there a limit to how much freedom of speech people should have?

Should neo-Nazis be allowed a platform to spread their views?

Should TV give extremist organisations a voice? Why/why not?

If you wish to set up debates like this, brainstorm ideas and write useful collocations on the board before the discussion itself begins. You can also then consolidate any discussion by setting a related topic as written homework.

The short poem at the end is good for practising the contracted form *'ll*, which for some speakers can be difficult. It leads nicely in to the next exercise.

4 Pronunciation

Emphasise the importance of saying *'ll*, not *will*. *I'll see you later* is the normal, natural way of saying it, whereas *I will see you later* means something different, with its suggestion of contradiction or emphasis. Play all the sentences through once, with students reading silently as they listen. Play the recording a second time and stop after each example for choral and individual repetition. Ask students what they think the situations are in the sentences. For example, you might say *You'll regret it* after your friend has told you that she is going to have her fifth vodka and orange in an hour. You could even have pairs develop a mini-dialogue around these phrases and then act it out.

Using vocabulary

1 Collocations with *go*

Go is one of the most commonly used verbs in English, and this exercise helps students use it in several different expressions. You could start off by asking what expressions with *go* they know already and then get them to work through the first task. Here students are presented with three correct collocations and one incorrect one – much better than three incorrect and one correct! After comparing answers with a partner, students can use some of the expressions to talk about their own plans for the weekend. Encourage them to continue these conversations by asking further questions. For example:

What film are you going to see? Where's it playing?

Questions 7–11 can be used for further practice of some of the vocabulary in the first task. You could suggest that students devote a whole page in their notebooks to expressions with *go*.

Answers

The wrong collocations are:

1. shopping tonight
2. my friend up in Yorkshire (Your students might ask about *up in Yorkshire*. Ask where they think the speaker is geographically (in the south of England).)
3. shopping
4. the pub
5. driving
6. some shopping

---

2 Vocabulary check

You could ask students straight away to explain the difference between *meeting, appointment* and *date*. However, it will probably be difficult for them. Ask them the question again after they have completed the three tasks. Hopefully, they will see that knowing each word's collocations helps explain the difference. You *have a meeting with your boss* or *with clients* – the word *meeting* is usually work-related. You'd usually *make/have an appointment with a dentist, doctor* or *optician*, although if you're going to an office to see a particular person, you might *have an appointment*. You *go on/have a date with* someone you're attracted to.

As you check the answers with the class, try to elicit other possible endings for each of the sentence beginnings. For example, in number 1 we might also say *with Dr Jones for five o'clock* or *with the optician tomorrow*, but we certainly wouldn't say *with a friend of mine later*. Encourage students to write down whole expressions with the words *meeting, appointment* and *date* in their notebooks. Explain that remembering natural examples is just as important as remembering what words mean. Refer students to the **Real English** note on page 53 for more on the expression *a friend's*.

Answers

1. c.   2. d.   3. a.   4. b.   5. f.   6. e.   7. h.   8. g.

---

3 Speaking

This exercise gives students a chance to personalise some of the vocabulary presented in **2 Vocabulary check**. You may wish to provide a couple of examples that are true for you, just to model the kind of language students can use. For example:

I've only been on one blind date in my life. A friend of mine set it up. We arranged to meet at this little Italian café I know. Anyway, I got there first and I was feeling pretty nervous. Then this gorgeous man/woman comes up to me and says, Hello, I haven't seen your teeth for a while. My blind date turned out to be my dentist!

Let students discuss the questions in small groups.

4 | Plan a weekend

This is a fun chance for students to put some of the grammar and vocabulary they have learned in this unit into practice. Before doing these tasks, get them to read the tapescript of Gavin's weekend plans on page 151 again to remind them of the kind of language they will need when telling others about their plans. Also give them useful language to make suggestions like:

Why don't we ... ?

Would you like to ... ?

Shall we ... ?

I'd really like to ...

In the first task, students work in pairs planning the ideal weekend. (The ideas in the Coursebook are just suggestions.) Then they should form new pairs and tell their new partner about this ideal weekend. Then, staying with their current partner, students work on the next task: planning a cheap weekend. Once they have come up with a plan, they should form another new pair and tell their new partner about their plan for the cheap weekend. When students are reporting the plans, they will probably need to use the present continuous and *going to,* and so you will be able to assess how well they are using these structures. Round up the activity by focusing on some common errors in a general class feedback session.

5 | Festivals

Use the photographs of *Samhuinn* to start a discussion on the topic of festivals. Here are some possible questions you could have students discuss:

Have you heard of Hallowe'en before?

Is there anything similar in your culture to mark the beginning of winter? How about the beginning of spring?

Do you have festivals where people dress up or paint their faces like this?

What are the most interesting festivals in your own country, region or town?

Is traditional culture still important to people in your country or region? What does it mean to you personally? Is it used to sell your country as a tourist destination? Give some examples.

These photos also provide an opportunity for students to practise the structure *they look* + adjective. Ask them to write down three possible endings to this sentence to describe the people in the pictures and to then compare their answers. For example:

They look brilliant/a bit scary/very serious/quite young.

6 | Idioms focus

To make this easier, have students work in groups. Have them translate and record the idioms they like in their notebooks. Here are some explanations if needed:

- You say *long time no see* when you meet someone you haven't seen for a relatively long time.
- You say *talk of the devil* when the person about whom you are talking suddenly shows up.
- You say *beggars can't be choosers* when you end up with an option that isn't what you wanted but which is better than nothing.
- You say *rather you than me* when someone tells you that they are going to do something that you wouldn't like to do.
- You say *there's no time like the present* to mean *now* when someone asks you when a good time to do something would be.
- You say *you must be joking* in response to someone who has said something unbelievable or unreasonable.

Answers
a. see
b. devil
c. choosers
d. me
e. present
f. joking
1. Long time no see
2. no time like the present
3. Rather you than me
4. talk of the devil
5. Beggars can't be choosers
6. You must be joking

8 Party animals

Language strip

Have students choose any expressions they find interesting and, on their own, find out more about them. In a later class, ask them to share the information. For a small group activity, ask students to divide the expressions into two groups: those most likely to be said by a person giving the party (e.g. *The food's over there*) and those most likely to be said by a guest (e.g. *Do you know anyone else here?*). Some expressions could fit either category. You might need to explain some of the following expressions:

- If you *feel like a fish out of water,* you feel uncomfortable because you are somewhere unfamiliar. For example: *My boyfriend once took me to a fancy garden party. I felt like a fish out of water.*

- You say *the night is still young* when you want to say there is a lot more time to do a lot more things before going to sleep. For example: *The pubs may have closed but the night is still young. Let's go to that new club.*

Lead in

You can use the pictures at the bottom of page 54 to bring up the subject of parties. Ask students to describe what kind of party is shown in each one. Follow up by asking further questions:

- *Have you ever been to a party like this? When was the last party you went to? What kind of party was it?*

- *Do you like going to parties?*

- *What do you like to do at parties? Dance, talk, eat, drink?*

- You may want to keep in mind that alcohol consumption may be a sensitive topic for some students.

Using vocabulary

1 What kind of party?

This exercise provides an opportunity for students to discuss different kinds of parties. Go through the list and ask some quick questions to check that students understand what each of the parties involves:

- *What should you wear for a fancy dress party?*
- *Why would you have a farewell party/house-warming party?*

There are also **Real English** notes for *a rave* and *stag night/hen night.* Write some verb collocations – *have a party, go to parties, give a dinner party* – on the board to help students while they are discussing. (There are more collocations in **2 Party collocations**.) Encourage students to talk in detail about what each kind of party involves for them personally. For example:

- *What happens when you have a big family get-together?*
- *Where would it usually be?*
- *Who comes?*
- *Is there food? Drink?*
- *How often do you have family get-togethers?*

You might want to talk about a party yourself first to give students the idea.

2 Party collocations

As well as the verbs *have* and *go to,* there are several other useful verb collocations for *party*. Students could work individually or in pairs. While going through the answers, ask further questions. For example in number 2, you could ask:

What do you think 'dumped' means?

Have you ever been dumped by your boyfriend/girlfriend in front of a crowd of people?

How would you translate 'dumped' into your own language?

Encourage students to add the collocations that they might need to their notebooks.

Answers

1. went on 2. ruined 3. broke up 4. gatecrash
5. finish 6. invite 7. throw 8. sorted out
---

3 Speaking

These questions give further practice using some of the vocabulary from **1 What kind of party?** and **2 Party collocations**. Talk about a personal experience first and encourage the class to ask you questions. For example:

We had this party once when I was at university, and all these gatecrashers turned up and started drinking all the beer, so a whole group of us decided to leave and go and gatecrash this other party that was going on down the road … .

This lets students hear the language you use before trying it themselves.

4 Planning a party

First, get each student to individually rank the items on the list (1 for most important, and so on). Before getting the students into pairs to compare and explain their order, write some sentence starters on the board to help them:

Well, for me personally, the most important thing is … because …

What I like is …

What I don't like is …

5 Planning expressions

In this exercise, students are introduced to some examples of expressions used while planning a party. They will then be able to use some of them in the role play in the next exercise (**6 Role play**). First, have students work on the ordering task, either in pairs or individually. Then have them underline the planning expressions. Write the expressions in order on the board, and where appropriate, show how other words could fit in:

I'll bring some (music/friends/CDs) if you sort out the (food/decorations/invitations).

How does that sound?

Well, to be honest, I'd rather organise the (food/music/invites), if it's OK with you.

Couldn't you do the (food/inviting/cleaning)?

Yeah, OK, no problem.

I'll try and bring some (music/crisps/wine).

What about the (invites/children/neighbours)?

Oh, I'll do that/those.

I'm looking forward to it already.

Answers

The correct order is:
1. a.   2. d.   3. c.   4. e.   5. b.
---

6 Role play

As well as being a fun activity, this is a chance for students to re-use some of the previously presented language. While they are discussing the first five questions in pairs, encourage the use of some of the expressions from **5 Planning expressions**. Before students walk around inviting each other, go over the questions they should ask (e.g. *Whereabouts is it?*) and remind them of some of the expressions used to turn down invitations from the role play on page 51. For example:

Oh, I'd love to, but I'm afraid I can't.

Well, I would if I could, but I can't.

Some appropriate responses are:

That's a shame.

Oh, well, maybe next time.

To add to the mood, you may want to play some party music in the background while students are chatting and circulating!

7 Speaking

The questions here allow students to share their ideas about presents, which can vary greatly from culture to culture. Have them work in small groups to talk about the questions. The picture at the bottom of page 55 can be used to extend the discussion. Students first need to decide what the object is, which is a great opportunity to use the very useful word *thing* and to practise language for describing objects and their position:
What's that yellow thing that looks a bit like a ship? (a butter dish)
What's that black thing with the orange circle? (a lighter for a gas cooker)
What's that thing in front of it? (an egg timer)

Write these examples on the board so that students know how to ask you while they are talking.

If they want to guess what the objects are, encourage the use of *might*. For example:
I'm not sure but it might be a spaghetti holder.

They can then talk about whether they would like to get any of the objects as presents. You could also talk about appropriate expressions to use if they ever got such a present:
What an interesting present. What do you use it for?

Other objects in the picture include the following:
The orange thing in the middle is a sellotape dispenser.
The thing behind it is a salad dressing set.
The thing in front of the sellotape dispenser is a stapler.
The silver thing on the right is an ashtray.

Reading

1 Collocations

While going through the answers here, ask for and provide further collocations. Also ask questions to generate connected language.

Answers
1. ended in tragedy
2. lose control
3. got out of hand
4. organised crime
5. led to calls for tighter laws
6. suffering from shock

2 Before you read

Have students try to predict what the article is about from the title and the six collocations in the task above.

3 While you read (Rave to the grave)

Have students read the article to see if their predictions were right and then share their reactions in pairs. Write a few sentence starters on the board for giving personal responses to the text. For example:
I can't believe that …

I think that the worst/funniest/most frightening thing about this article is the fact that …

4 Comprehension check

This task helps reinforce several collocations from the article. Have students correct the sentences without looking back at the text and then ask them to compare their answers with a partner. If there are differences, they can then refer back to the text.

Answers
1. The party was held in a deserted flat (on a housing estate in East London).
2. (The extremely high volume of) the techno music being played weakened the structure of the floor.
3. Bert Jones is waiting for the council to send someone round to fix his flat.
4. There have been a number of complaints about techno parties all over the capital.
5. The number of drug-related deaths at raves has risen dramatically over the last year.
6. Most of the young people just carried on dancing when the floor collapsed.

5 | Speaking

You could introduce the task by telling the class about a noisy or wild party you have been to. Have the class talk about the questions in small groups. You could easily develop the questions into debates or written homework. For example:

What could or should be done about drug-taking?

Do you think 'soft' drugs should be decriminalised?

Should the police concentrate more on organised crime than on drug-takers?

If you use any of these, give students a list of useful expressions and collocations beforehand. For example:

a rise in recreational drug use

We should differentiate between hard and soft drug use.

call for tougher sentences

put more money into drug awareness campaigns

It's a complex issue.

6 | I just couldn't wait

Just is another word which is better to learn in expressions. Here it is part of a sentence starter *I just couldn't …* . After discussing why Bert Jones said *I just couldn't believe it* (his living room was full of dust and plaster and people screaming), point out that *just* here is used for emphasis. After students have completed the task and checked their answers, have them practise saying the phrases, paying attention to the stress patterns. As always, encourage students to record examples of these expressions in context in their notebooks.

Answers

1. c. I just couldn't wait
2. e. I just couldn't believe my eyes
3. a. I just couldn't make up my mind
4. b. I just couldn't bear it any longer
5. d. I just couldn't resist them

---

7 | Speaking

Tell the class a personal story first and encourage them to ask you questions before having them talk in small groups. These questions provide an opportunity to use the *I just couldn't* expressions above. You could extend this activity by getting pairs to write and perform a skit based on one of these situations, for example, a couple who can't decide where to go for their holiday.

Photo opportunity

You could use the photo on page 56 to talk about fashion or the topic of dance music. (*What kind of music do you like to dance to? What kind of music is hard to dance to?*)

Using vocabulary

1 | Party politics

The focus here shifts to politics and the law. You could make the connection by asking the class to tell you about the attitudes politicians take to youth culture, like raves, in their country/countries. Go through the questions first, drawing attention to the highlighted collocations. Then get the students to ask each other the questions. If you are from a different country from your students, you might want to tell them about the party system or political situation in your country. Remind students to add the collocations that they like to their notebooks.

2 | Do, make

This task gives more examples of these two verbs, some in the context of politics. If students already have pages set aside in their notebooks for expressions with *do* and *make*, have them add these expressions to those pages.

Answers

1. make 2. do 3. made 4. made 5. make 6. make
7. do 8. do, make 9. do 10. make 11. make 12. do

You may want to explain the following expressions:

- If you *want to make the most of your time somewhere,* you want to use the time well and not waste it. For example*: You should make the most of your time here by visiting the museums and galleries.*

- If you *make an effort to do something,* you try hard to do it. For example: *Please make an effort to be on time.*

- If something *doesn't do anything for you,* you don't understand why other people like it. For example: *I know lots of people like it, but folk music doesn't really do anything for me.*

3 Talking about the law

The first part of this activity focuses on the collocation *introduce a new law* and associated verbs. Other verb collocations with *law* appear in the second part. Have students match the sentence halves and go through the answers. While you are checking, ask further questions like:

Do you think they should ban smoking in public places?

What kind of laws would help protect the environment?

They here is a 'dummy subject' and this structure is an alternative to the traditional passive. Explain that if *people are given tax breaks,* their taxes are reduced for a particular reason. For example, you might get a tax break if you buy a fuel-efficient car.

Answers
1. b.   2. d.   3. a.   4. c.   5. f.   6. h.   7. e.   8. g.

4 Role play

For this activity, get students into groups of three (or four). Explain the decisions that they need to make and give them some useful language to help them:

I think it's important for us to …

We'll get a lot of support if we …

Banning/Legalising … will be a vote-winner.

One way to handle the campaigning is to have one person act as the spokesperson and let them briefly present their party's policies in front of the class. After allowing time for questions, you can conduct the elections. Be as simple or elaborate as you want. You might want to talk about different voting systems such as *first past the post* and *proportional representation.*

5 Political quotes

The quotations here can be the basis for discussion or for a writing task on the role of the media in politics, the nature of power, or the use or non-use of violence for political ends. Ask students if they have some favourite political quotations to share with the rest of the class. You could ask students if there are any political leaders they admire and why. Are these leaders good public speakers?

Photo opportunity

Use the pictures on page 59 to ask questions. For example:

Do you recognise these politicians?

Do you ever see politicians on demonstrations?

Have you ever been on a demonstration yourself? If so, what was the demonstration about?

How do politicians usually campaign during an election? Do they go around shaking hands, kissing babies?

Review: Units 5–8

The exercises here can be used as a quiz. **5 Look back and check: Adjectives**, however, is better done as a discussion in pairs.

1 Tenses

Answers

1. I hadn't	6. We hadn't been
2. I'd	7. We're going
3. I'm meeting	8. I were
4. I hadn't been feeling	9. Will you
5. I'll	10. I've got to

2 Multiple choice

Answers

1. a.   2. b.   3. b.   4. a.   5. a.   6. a.   7. b.   8. a.
9. a.   10. a.

3 Conditionals

Answers

1. e.   2. a.   3. f.   4. b.   5. c.   6. d.

4 Conversation

Answers

1. a.   2. e.   3. g.   4. d.   5. h.   6. c.   7. f.   8. i.
9. b.

5 Look back and check: Adjectives

Answers will vary.

6 Expressions

Answers

1. I just felt like it.
2. What a nightmare
3. I would if I could
4. You'll regret it
5. That's a good question
6. make up my mind

7 Collocations

Answers

1. e.   2. h.   3. f.   4. a.   5. j.   6. d.   7. c.   8. b.
9. g.   10. i.   11. r.   12. q.   13. o.   14. l.   15. m.
16. n.   17. k.   18. p.

8 Real English

Answers

1. e.   2. b.   3. a.   4. f.   5. d.   6. c.

9 Idioms

Answers

1. e.   2. f.   3. a.   4. b.   5. h.   6. d.   7. c.   8. g.

10 What can you remember?

Answers will vary.

11 Vocabulary quiz

Answers

1. It means you can't find them anywhere.
2. Answers will vary.
3. Yes, because you're not allowed to smoke on board planes.
4. You didn't do anything special.
5. *Left-wing* is liberal/socialist while *right-wing* is conservative.
6. Answers will vary. Your neighbours could break up a party if it's too loud. The police could break up a party if the neighbours complain about the noise.
7. An appointment.
8. I wouldn't eat a frog if you paid me.
9. Have dinner there.
10. You smoke too much.
11. If you *go shopping*, it's for fun things like clothes or shoes or CDs or whatever. If you *do the shopping*, you buy all the things you use every day – milk, bread, sugar, and so on.
12. At the end.
13. It takes forever.
14. Yes, you can be on board a boat.
15. They could tighten laws on drinking by imposing fines or punishments. They could tighten laws on immigration by making it more difficult for people to come and live in a country.
16. Yes, your relations and relatives are the same.
17. You go on a day-trip.
18. A court.
19. It's small, warm, secure and friendly-looking.
20. On a plane.

Learner advice: The authors speak!

Answers will vary.

9 Last night

Unit overview

General topic

Talking about what you did last night.

Dialogue

Lucy tells Rose about her night at the worst disco in town. Rose tells Lucy about her quiet night at home.

Language input

- Expressions to describe how your night was: *I didn't know a single person there, I met loads of interesting people there*, etc.

- Collocations with *get*: *get a taxi, get wet, get lost*, etc.

- Differentiating similar words and phrases: *chat/talk, gossiped/talked*, etc.

- Responding with auxiliary verbs: *Did you? Have you?* etc.

- Asking for repetition: *You went where?*

- Not … until … : *I didn't get in until three.*

- Linking cause-effect ideas with *so* + adjective: *The music was so loud, I couldn't hear myself think.*

Language strip

Have students choose any expressions they find interesting and, on their own, find out more about them. In a later class, ask them to share the information. For a small group activity, ask them to find expressions that fit into the following categories: expressions that they might use if they were talking about a great time (e.g. *You'd have enjoyed yourself, It's the place to be*) and ones they might use if they were talking about a bad time (e.g. *The food was awful, What a bore!*). Ask students to suggest answers for the expressions containing questions. For example:

A: *Who did you say you bumped into?*
B: *My old maths teacher.*

You might need to explain some of the following expressions:

- If somewhere is *not really your sort of place*, it is somewhere you feel uncomfortable or don't usually go. For example: *Wine bars are not really my sort of place.*

- You describe a person as *a bore* when they aren't interesting or don't want to do something that you want to do. For example: *He goes to bed at 9:30 even on Fridays. He's such a bore!*

- If you *bump into someone*, you meet them by chance. For example: *If you happen to bump into Bob later, could you tell him to call me?*

- If something *was a rip-off*, you had to pay too much for it and/or the quality wasn't good. For example: *£5 for an ice cream? What a rip-off!*

- If something *is out of this world*, you are stressing that it is very good. For example: *You have to try their passion fruit ice cream. It's out of this world.*

Lead in

You can lead in to the topic by talking about what you did last night and then ask the class to go around asking each other. Once students have talked to several people, stop them and ask questions like:
Tell me about someone who had a quiet night in/went out for a drink/did something unusual.

Using vocabulary

1 Lifestyle

First, have students discuss in pairs what kind of lifestyle they lead. Before getting them to talk about whether they ever do any of the ten activities listed, elicit several frequency expressions and write them on the board. For example: *once in a while, hardly ever, every other day.* You could also check whether anyone actually did any of these activities last night.

Explain that they are going to hear four people talking about what they did last night. For each person, they should choose the activity they did from the list. You probably only need to play the recording once for this task, but you might want to ask students to listen again for any useful expressions. Have them tell you what expressions they heard and write them on the board. Play the recording one more time as they follow the tapescript on page 151.

Answers

Speaker 1 went to the laundrette.
Speaker 2 went out for a walk around town.
Speaker 3 had a quiet night at home.
Speaker 4 went to her evening class.

---

2 | So how was your night?

You could lead in to this exercise by asking questions about any of the activities your students did last night:
You watched a film on TV? So how was it?
You went out for dinner last night? So how was the food?

Have students complete the ten sentences in pairs. While checking the answers, ask them to tell you what is being talked about. For example, number 1 might have been said about a party. Students should recognise some of the idioms from previous units (e.g. *out of my depth, we had nothing in common, get on like a house on fire*). Here are some others that you may need to explain:

- *Loads of* is an informal way of saying *a lot of*. For example: *Don't worry about the bill; she's got loads of money.*

- If you *take something up* seriously, you want to spend time doing it as a serious hobby. For example: *I want to take up kick-boxing seriously.*

- If you spend time *catching up with a friend*, you talk to them to find out what they have been doing since you last met. For example: *I'm going out with an old school friend who I haven't seen for twenty years, so we've got a lot of catching up to do.*

- If you *are on the edge of your seat*, you are very interested in something and want to see what happens next. For example: *This film will keep you on the edge of your seat right up until the end.*

> **Answers**
>
> 1. single 2. horrendous 3. absolutely 4. depth
> 5. halfway 6. house 7. loads 8. catch up
> 9. taking it up 10. seat

Draw students' attention to this pattern:
A: So how was … ?
B: I had a … time.

Then get them to practise asking and answering the questions a–e.

3 | Speaking

Tell the class about when you last had a great time or a terrible time. Encourage them to ask you questions and then to talk about their own experiences in pairs or small groups.

4 | Collocations with *get*

Start off by telling students that *get* is one of the most commonly used verbs in English, and that it is a good idea to record expressions with *get* on a separate page in their notebooks. Ask them to give you some examples before working on the exercise. After students have underlined the expressions with *get*, encourage them to record any that they like in their notebooks.

> **Answers**
>
> 1. my hair cut
> 2. money
> 3. a call
> 4. something to eat
> 5. upset
> 6. wet
> 7. surprise
> 8. a job
> 9. bus
> 10. lost
>
> The *get* expressions are:
> 1. I got my hair cut
> 2. I tried to get some money
> 3. I got a call from …
> 4. I … to get something to eat
> 5. I got really upset
> 6. I got really wet
> 7. I got a real surprise
> 8. I've finally got a job
> 9. I had to get the last bus home
> 10. I … ended up getting lost

For the next task write some possible sentence starters on the board to help students:
I get … when …
I got … last (night/week/year)
I'm hoping to get …

You could also ask them which expressions can have *very* added to them. (You can't *get very better, very married* or *very pregnant*, but all the others are possible.) You may want to add to the four questions that end this exercise in order to recycle some other vocabulary from the ten sentences: *When was the last time you got a big surprise/got really upset/got your hair cut?* etc. For homework, you could ask students to write a short story (about 100 words) called 'Last night' in which they have to use eight expressions with *get*. It can be as strange as they like (forcing the use of these expressions means it will inevitably be a little strange anyway).

5 | Problem words

This exercise focuses on the difference in meaning between closely related words and phrases. Have the class work in pairs for both tasks.

Answers

a. If you *have a chat*, it's usually with a friend and it's about nothing in particular. Your boss or your parents or your teacher might *have a talk with you*, and it's usually about a problem that needs to be sorted out or because you've done something wrong.

b. If you *gossiped about* the boss, you talked about all the rumours you'd heard: who they are dating, how they treat people, who said what to them and when, and so on. If you *talked about work*, it suggests you discussed business: how things are going at work, and so on.

c. If you *do the washing-up*, you wash the dirty dishes. If you *do the washing*, you wash dirty clothes.

d. *I went to a disco* is just a fact about what you did last night. *We ended up going to a disco* suggests you'd been to lots of other places first, and that the disco was the end of a very long evening out!

e. If you *miss the last bus home*, you don't catch it, and then maybe have to get a cab home, or walk! If you *miss a person*, you spend a lot of time thinking about them and longing for the day they return.

f. If you *go out after work*, you go for a drink or to the cinema, or you meet up with some friends and go out for dinner, or something like that. If you *leave work*, you just leave the building where you work.

1. I had a talk with her
2. I had a chat with her
3. We talked about work
4. We gossiped about the boss
5. I did the washing
6. I did the washing-up
7. we ended up going to a disco
8. I went to a disco
9. I missed the last bus home
10. I really missed her when she was in Spain
11. I left work last night about five
12. I went out last night after work

Listening

1 | Before you listen

Ask the class to talk about places they would never go to in the town or city they are in now or, if this is different, the town or city where they are from. Ask why they would never go there and whether this is based on experience.

2 | While you listen (The Worst Disco in Town!)

Explain that students are going to hear a conversation between two flatmates, Rose and Lucy, about what happened last night. Ask the class to suggest some possible scenarios based on the title. Go through the two questions and play the recording, asking students to listen for the answers. Remind them to cover the text. Get them to discuss their answers in pairs. Next, let them read the conversation as you play the recording again. Then ask them to fill in the first two or three gaps from memory in pairs, before you play the recording again, this time with pauses, so that they can check and fill in the missing words. Do this two or three gaps at a time until the end. Play the recording through one more time with students following the script. You may finally want students to read the conversation, or parts of it, in pairs, using the tapescript on page 152.

Answers

1. Rose did a bit of shopping on her way home, then cooked some Japanese noodles, did a bit of tidying up, read a bit, watched a film and then went to bed. Lucy went out with some old friends that she hadn't seen for ages. They had a drink and something to eat, and then they had another drink and eventually ended up going to this terrible disco, 'Stardust', where Lucy got chatted up by a much, much younger guy. She then missed the last train home and had to get a cab!

2. Rose went to bed after one. Lucy didn't get in until three, and must've gone to bed soon after!

Encourage students to notice, ask about and record in their notebooks any of the expressions they find interesting in the conversation. You might want to point out how Rose uses *did a bit of* several times as well as the expression *for a bit*.

Refer students to the two **Real English** notes on *I bet* and *get a cab*. You could ask them to guess things about the four people in the pictures on page 64 using *I bet …* (*I bet the man in picture C never goes to discos*). You could also point out that *I bet* is often used on its own as a way of agreeing or sympathising with the person we're talking to. For example:

A: *It was really funny when I told him I was thirty-five.*
B: *Yeah, I bet! He probably couldn't believe it.*

See if the class can write a dialogue like this in pairs. It is sometimes falsely believed that *taxi* is British English and *cab* is American English. In fact, both words are common in British English.

3 | Speaking

The questions here provide an opportunity for students to connect the content of the listening task to their own lives and experiences. Make sure that students know that if you *chat someone up*, you talk to someone because you are sexually attracted to them. Talk about any personal experiences for any of these questions either before or after the students talk about theirs.

Using grammar

1 | Responding with auxiliary verbs

This exercise focuses on a useful way of responding to what someone has said to show interest and to keep the conversation going. Make sure that students know what auxiliaries there are in English (forms of *do, be* and *have*, and modal auxiliaries). Ask the class to read the two examples first and then to follow as they listen to the recording. Point out how the auxiliary is stressed. Have students practise copying the responses chorally and individually before asking pairs to read the two mini-conversations.

Students can work individually on the next task. Explain that they should look at the dialogues 1–8 and add the correct auxiliary question in the first gap. Then they should choose the question or comment a–h. You might want to do the first dialogue as an example. After checking the answers, students can practise reading the eight short dialogues in pairs. Encourage them to add another comment to make three-line dialogues.

Refer students to the example dialogues to show what you mean. Here is an example for number 1:

A: *I'm a pretty good cook, believe it or not.*
B: *Are you? So when are you going to invite me round for dinner, then?*
A: *Oh, I don't know. Maybe sometime.*

Answers

1. Are you? + g
2. Have you? + b
3. Did you? + d
4. Were you? + f
5. Are you?/Do you? + e
6. Do you? + a
7. Would you? + h
8. Are you? + c

---

2 | Talking about you

This exercise gives students the chance to practise these responding techniques in an interpersonal context. To help students, write five sentences that are true for you on the board using the sentence starters. For example:
I can play the flute.
I'd really love to go to Venice.
Believe it or not, I've never been skiing.
When I was younger, I once ate a worm.
Last night I stayed out until three in the morning.

Then ask students to write five true sentences of their own. Next, get the class to respond to each of your sentences using an auxiliary question and a follow-up question. For example:
Can you? Why don't you play us a tune?

Continue the conversation as in the previous exercise:
Oh, well, I don't actually have the flute with me. It's back at my parents'.

Using this as a model, get the students to walk around the class sharing their sentences and responding to each other. Refer students to the **Grammar commentary, G11 Responding with auxiliary verbs** on page 162 so that they can review this pattern.

Photo opportunity

Use the photos on page 67 as a prompt for students to construct their own dialogues between two flatmates discussing what they did last night. Brainstorm lots of potential expressions and write them on the board. For example:

So what were you up to last night?

I didn't get in until …

Did you miss the bus?

Then give pairs of students time to prepare and practise their dialogues. You can finish off by having them perform their dialogues to other groups.

3 Making sure you understand

Introduce this exercise by asking what expressions or strategies your students use when they don't understand something someone has said to them. Give them an example by saying: *Before I became a teacher, I was a … .* Make sure that the end of your sentence is inaudible. Ask students how they would respond. You'll probably get *I beg your pardon. What? What did you say?* Explain that you are going to show them an technique in informal spoken English that focuses on the specific part of the statement that is not understood. Have them read the two examples and ask what pattern they notice. Say your sentence again and ask them to respond in a similar way: *You were what?* Play the recording so that they can hear the stress and intonation and then have them practise in pairs. Point out that in answering these questions the first speaker repeats the problem word and then explains what it means.

Answers

1. It cost what?/It cost how much?
2. You had dinner where?
3. You did what last night?
4. You arrived here when?
5. You went what?/You did what?
6. It cost how much?/It cost what?
7. You found a (baby) what?
8. You went where?

With a multi-lingual class, a fun way of extending this exercise is to ask students to write three sentences about themselves using one word or phrase from their own language. This word can be a food, a drink, a thing, a place, a kind of building, etc. Students then walk around class, telling each other their sentences, asking questions to clarify what the other person is talking about. For example:

A: *In my country, we often have nasi goreng for breakfast.*

B: *You have what for breakfast?*

A: *Nasi goreng. It's a kind of fried rice dish. It's really nice.*

Refer students to the **Real English** note on *grand* and *quid*. Explain that the plurals are the same, *grand* and *quid*.

4 Not until

This structure is used to emphasise that something happened later than expected or later than usual. See if students are able to explain why Lucy used this phrase before you explain to them. They can then work on sentences 1–8 individually and compare answers in pairs.

Answers

1. b.   2. a.   3. a.   4. a.   5. b.   6. b.   7. a.   8. b.

5 Discuss

In this exercise students can make up answers if they want. Remind them that they should only use *I didn't … until* if it is appropriate. Encourage them to ask further questions like: *Why? What were you doing? Why so late?* Tell the class to read the **Grammar commentary, G12 not … until …** on page 162, to review this structure.

6 Linking ideas

This exercise focuses on a very common way of expressing cause and effect in spoken English. The examples in the exercise are typical expressions, so you could ask the class to try and learn all eight sentences by heart. Play the recording so that they can hear how *so* is stressed. One way to practise the phrases is in pairs, with one person reading the first half of the sentence and the other completing the other half from memory.

Answers

1. g.   2. e.   3. h.   4. c.   5. f.   6. a.   7. b.   8. d.

To review these expressions in a later class, write each half of the sentence on a slip of paper. Repeat some of them so that you have about four more slips than the total number of students in your class. Shuffle the slips and give each student one, keeping the extras yourself. Ask students to memorise their half of the sentence and then to go around saying it until they find their matching half. When they have found their partner, tell them to return the slips to you and to each take another slip from the pile. This way you can keep recycling the phrases. This is a fast activity that shouldn't take longer than five minutes.

7 More conversations

Let students generate their own ideas in pairs and practise saying the conversations. Accept their answers if they sound OK to you, but when finishing up the task, you might want to point out that there are fairly predictable ways of ending most of these sentences too.

Answers

Possible endings:

1. (… it was so bad,) I walked out halfway through/after half an hour.

2. (It was so delicious,) I'm going to go back again tonight/I ate more than I should have.

3. (I was so exhausted, I) was in bed by nine/I just went straight to bed as soon as I got in.

4. (Terrible, it was so) boring/long/dull, (I) nearly fell asleep in the middle of it/I wish I hadn't gone at all.

5. (I got so) annoyed about everything, (I) couldn't tell him how I really feel about things/I just stormed out/I got so upset, I just burst into tears.

6. (I was so) nervous, (I) just messed the whole thing up/I couldn't concentrate.

Get students to follow up by reading the **Grammar commentary, G13 Linking ideas** on page 162, and by adding the expressions they like to their notebooks.

Photo opportunity

As a lead-in to the role play, ask students what they think is happening in the photo on page 69. For example: *What kind of questions might the police be asking?*

Has anything like this ever happened to you? What happened?

8 Role play

Explain that the purpose of this exercise is to review in a light-hearted way some of the language from the unit (for example, talking about last night: *I had an early night*; responding with auxiliaries: *Where were you? What were you doing there?* etc.). Explain the situation. Have the class decide on the two suspects and give them all between five and ten minutes to prepare their stories and questions. During the interviews, make a note of any vocabulary or grammar problems that arise. Round up the activity by writing these mistakes on the board and ask students to correct or improve them.

Unit overview

General topic

Relationships and describing what you like in a partner.

Reading

Two examples of mixed marriages: different religions and different ages.

Language input

- Using *look: He looks like a model, She looks as if she's about to collapse*, etc.
- Adjectives for describing character and appearance: *down-to-earth, muscular*, etc.
- Using *I bet* to make guesses: *I bet he's studying Chemistry or something*.
- Fixed expressions with modals: *I could've told you that, You can say that again*, etc.
- Tend to: *Men tend to eat more junk food than women*.

Language strip

Have students choose any expressions they find interesting and, on their own, find out more about them. In a later class, ask them to share the information. For a small group activity, ask students to find expressions that show a preference (e.g. *I prefer older men, I only like people with money*) and to talk about whether they have the same preferences. Alternatively, they can find expressions that could be used by two friends talking about the partner of one of them (e.g. *I don't know what you see in her, He's old enough to be your father*).

Encourage students to record the expressions that they like in their notebooks. You might need to explain some of the following expressions:

- You might say *Where've you been all my life?* to someone you have just met and find attractive. It's a clichéd chat-up line in British English.
- You can describe a young man as *a bit of a lad* if he enjoys having a laugh with his friends. Recently though, *lad culture* or *laddish behaviour* has come to be a negative way of describing macho, sexist, aggressive, unruly and offensive young men.
- You would say *You can get lost* or *Go jump in the river* to someone who was annoying you and you wanted them to go away. Both are fairly strong.
- If you say *we've decided to go our separate ways*, it means that you and your partner are splitting up.

- If you say *I don't know what you see in her/him*, you mean that you don't understand why your friend is in a relationship with this person because his/her character or appearance is not appealing.

Lead in

You can lead in to the topic of relationships by referring back to the story of Rose and Lucy in Unit 9. Ask questions like:
What do you think a teenager would see in an older woman?
What would an older woman see in a teenager?
What do you think the teenager said to Rose to get her to dance?

Using grammar

1 Judging by appearances

In this exercise students are introduced to three structures that follow the verb *look*. Some students have problems knowing when to use *like* after *look,* so give them plenty of practice. Introduce the task by asking whether they find any of the people in the photo on page 70 attractive. Have them explain why/why not. Then explain that they should complete the nine sentences with either *looks, looks like* or *looks as if.* When they have finished, ask them to tell you the guideline for using these structures:
look + adjective
look like + noun
look as if + clause/statement

You could also mention that in spoken English *as if* is sometimes replaced with *like*. As you are checking the answers, ask questions to check that students understand the sentences and to generate further language. For example in number 9:
How could you tell if someone is down?
What kind of things might cause you to look a bit down?

Point out the **Real English** note that explains *creep* and *nerd*.

2 Speaking

Have students discuss whether any of the sentences in **1 Judging by appearances** could describe any of the people pictured at the bottom of the page. Encourage them to use *He/she looks …* and to add any other descriptions that they think apply. Finish off by having the whole class share their ideas. Tell students to read the **Grammar commentary, G14 Judging by appearances** on page 162 to review these structures.

Using vocabulary

1 Descriptive adjectives

In this exercise students work on building up their vocabulary to describe people. Explain that in the first task they are to sort the adjectives according to whether they describe character, appearance or both. You might want to do the first two as an example. In the next task they are to decide whether the adjectives are positive or negative. It is important to remind students that this is often a personal opinion. However, certain words, like *pushy*, are more commonly used negatively, while others, like *dishy*, are generally positive. It is possible that some students find the idea of *muscular*, *dishy* men appealing, while others do not. Have pairs compare their ideas. You may need to explain some of the adjectives here:

- If someone is *pushy*, they try to get what they want in a forceful or insistent way. For example: *He's very pushy; he's always asking when I'm going to be ready to settle down and have kids.*

- If someone is *forward*, they are not shy or hesitant about something. For example: *You're very forward coming up and asking me to come back to your place.*

- If you describe someone as *down-to-earth*, you like the fact that they are concerned with practical things rather than abstract ideas.

- If someone is *flirty*, they act as if they are sexually attracted to other people, usually in a playful sort of way.

Point out the **Real English** note for *dishy*.

Have students work in pairs describing other people in the class. You can write sentence starters like *I think he/she is quite/a bit … , I think he/she seems …* on the board to help. As an extension, bring in some personal advertisements from the newspaper: *Tall, dark, handsome man in late twenties seeks large, cuddly, mature lady for friendship*, etc. Look at a few together as a class and deal with any new words and expressions. Then ask students to write their own personal advertisement. Put them up on the wall at the end of class. Perhaps somebody will find their dream partner!

2 I bet

Remind students of how Lucy used *I bet* in Unit 9 to make a guess about something she was fairly sure about: *I bet he hadn't even started shaving.* Go over the examples, having students practise saying them. Write the pattern on the board:
A: *He/she looks …*
B: *I know. I bet he/she …*

They can then use this as a guide for talking about the people in the photos at the bottom of page 71. For example:
A: *The man in the picture looks quite muscular.*
B: *I know. I bet he works as a bouncer or something.*

3 Chat-up lines

This exercise provides some light relief, but it also introduces students to typical culturally-specific chat-up lines, and thus guards students against them in future! Many students may not realise, for example, that number 1 is a classic chat-up line, whereas to most native speakers it would be very obvious. It may be both amusing and educational to put the class into male/female pairs to compare the best/worst chat-up lines! Students could discuss which might be said by a female and which by a male. You could also work on ways to tell someone you are not interested. For example:
I'm waiting for my boyfriend/girlfriend. Do I look desperate?

The questions at the end of the exercise could be discussed in the same pairs or in small groups.

Reading

1 What turns you on?

This is a ranking activity to generate some discussion leading in to the reading task. Have students work through the list individually first and then compare their answers with a partner. Suggest that they do two sets of rankings: one for what is important in *a partner*, the other for *a friend*. Check that they know that *partner* here means someone you are in a sexual relationship with. The discussion is a good way to review comparative structures and *-ing* forms. Write some phrases on the board to help them in the discussion. For example:

Being/Having … is more important than being/having … .

I'd rather have someone who is/can … than someone who is/can … .

2 Prepositions

Prepositions are notorious among learners of English because it seems there are no useful rules to explain their use. Advise students to learn and record prepositions as they are used in phrases. This exercise may prove difficult, so have students work in pairs or small groups. You may want them to use dictionaries so that they get into the habit of finding appropriate prepositions (and collocations) when they want to use a word. The prepositional phrases here also appear in the reading text, so ask students to predict what the text will be about by looking at the title. As you go through the sentences, ask questions to generate further language. For example:

Have you ever had to break some bad news to someone?

Have your parents ever disapproved of someone you were going out with?

Remind students to record some of these prepositional phrases in their notebooks.

Answers

1. to 2. of 3. with 4. for 5. of 6. with

---

3 Before you read

Write *mixed marriage* on the board and ask what students think this means (usually it refers to a marriage between people of different races or religions, but as you will see it could refer to different generations or classes!). You could then discuss what the advantages and disadvantages of a mixed marriage might be.

4 While you read (Is she really going out with him?)

Students can read the article to find out if any of the ideas they discussed in **3 Before you read** were mentioned. You may want to read the text aloud or play the recorded version to the students as they follow in their Coursebooks. Listening and reading at the same time shows students how language is grouped together in chunks. Hearing appropriately 'chunked' language helps students learn to listen for and use words in groups, thus aiding overall fluency. Once students have read the article, have them share their initial reactions in pairs. Here are some words and expressions students might ask about:

- If you *are ostracised*, it means that people do not allow you to be a part of their lives because of something you have done.

- *My mates* means *my friends*. Sometimes people use the word *mate* to address someone directly: *Hello, mate, All right, mate?* It is normally used by men to talk about or talk to other men.

- If someone *has just turned sixty*, it means that they have just had their sixtieth birthday.

5 After reading

Use the first two questions (the first two tasks) to extend the discussion about the article. Questions 1–5 in the third task focus on comprehension. Have pairs of students discuss their answers without looking at the text. They can then reread the article to confirm their answers.

Answers

1. Jamie and Jane. (When Jamie's parents met Jane, they got on really well.)

2. David and Rachel. (As Rachel and David know, people in mixed marriages are often verbally abused.)

3. David and Rachel. ('We actually found it difficult to find a place to live in Belfast because areas tend to be either Catholic or Protestant.')

4. Jamie and Jane. ('Jane often stays in with my parents when I go out clubbing.')

5. David and Rachel. (As Rachel and David know, people in mixed marriages are often ostracised.)

---

6 | Word check

This exercise focuses on several collocations in the text. Remind students to add those they find useful to their notebooks. Students can either do this individually or in pairs. Have them try to complete the phrases from memory first and then to look in the text. To make it easier, give them the paragraph references. When you check their answers, ask further questions to check their understanding and to generate connected language. For example:

Are mixed marriages becoming increasingly common in your country?

Have your parents ever put pressure on you to do something?

Answers

1. increasingly (common) (paragraph 1)
2. (family) pressure (paragraph 1)
3. (got a lot of) support from (paragraph 2)
4. cloakroom (paragraph 3)
5. (typical macho) lad (paragraph 3)
6. (find that kind of man very) appealing (paragraph 4)

Refer students to the **Real English** note on *pulling my leg*. Ask whether anyone likes *pulling people's legs* or whether they like *their legs being pulled*.

Using vocabulary

1 | Speaking

Be sensitive to students' views and personal experiences when you discuss this kind of topic. Students are entitled not to join in discussions which make them feel uncomfortable. If possible and appropriate, put the class in mixed-sex groups for the discussion. Before they start, allow them a couple of minutes to read through all the questions and to ask you about anything that is not clear. Tell them they don't have to answer all the questions and are free to skip any they are not comfortable with. If the class enjoys discussing some of these questions, ask them to choose one and write about it for homework.

2 | Stages of a relationship

Students can work individually and then compare their answers with a partner. Point out the expressions with *get*: *getting married, just got engaged, getting divorced.* You can use this exercise to ask about traditions of getting engaged (e.g. *Do you exchange rings? How long is the engagement period? Is there a party?*), or the mechanics of getting a divorce (e.g. *What do you need to do to get a divorce? Is it difficult to get a divorce? Is there a high divorce rate?*). Note that you usually decide to *separate* before officially *getting divorced.*

Answers

A possible order is:

1. d.   2. g.   3. c.   4. b.   5. f. (or e.)   6. e. (or f.)
7. a.   8. h.

Using grammar

1 | Expressions with modals

The use of modals is another area that causes learners of English a lot of problems. Deciding which modal to use depends on the speaker's attitude to the event being described, thus allowing for a lot of variation. In this exercise, however, the focus is on fixed expressions where there really is only one choice. Encourage students to record the complete expression. Let students try to complete sentences 1–9 on their own, and then compare with a partner before you check their answers. They can then try to complete the expressions at the bottom of the page from memory. You might need to explain some expressions in this task:

- If you say *something is common knowledge*, you think it is a well-known fact. For example: *I thought it was common knowledge that they were living together.*

- You say *You can say that again* when you agree with something someone has just said.

- You say *You must be joking* when you think that what someone has said is unreasonable or unbelievable.

- If you say *And pigs might fly* about something, you don't believe it will ever happen.

Answers

1. could 2. can 3. should 4. must 5. must 6. could
7. couldn't 8. must 9. might

The expressions are:

1. That must've been nice.
2. You can say that again!
3. You must be joking!
4. You must be mad!
5. I just couldn't believe it!
6. I could've told you that.
7. I could hardly hear myself think!
8. You should've known better!
9. Pigs might fly!

---

2 | Grammar in context

This exercise recycles some of the expressions from
1 Expressions with modals in new contexts. Practise
the pronunciation of the expressions so that students
feel comfortable saying them. You could then ask
students in pairs to have two-line conversations, with
one student using sentences 1–5 as prompts and the
other adding the appropriate phrase. As an extension
you could ask pairs to write nine more dialogues using
these nine expressions in context.

Answers

Probable answers are:

1. That must've been nice.
2. You should've known better (after what happened
    last time)/I could've told you that!
3. You can say that again/I know. I could hardly hear
    myself think!
4. You can say that again/I know! I just couldn't
    believe it!
6. You must be joking! (It was rubbish.)

---

3 | I could do with ...

This exercise practises another modal expression that
students may remember from Unit 9. After looking at
the example, ask the class what they think *I could do with*
means (an informal way of saying *I would like/I wish I had*).
Have students work on the exercise individually and
then compare answers and talk about other things they
could do with at the moment with a partner. Round up by
writing the following on the board and ask students to
tell each other in pairs which ones are true for them:

I could do with a drink.

I could do with a break.

I could do with a haircut.

I could do with some new clothes.

Encourage students to have short conversations like
this:

A: *I could do with a drink.*

B: *Me too. Shall I go and get a couple of coffees?*

A: *Well, that wasn't the kind of drink I had in mind.*

Answers

1. I could do with some help
2. I could do with something to eat
3. I could do with a break
4. I could do with a bit more time
5. I could do with a holiday
6. I could do with a lie-in
7. I could do with a good night's sleep
8. I could do with more money

Tell the class to read the **Grammar commentary,
G15 Expressions with modals** on page 162, for more
on the basic meaning of some modal verbs.

Using vocabulary

1 | Tend to

Tend to, whilst not being traditionally classified as a
modal, is often used to make statements more tentative
in a similar way as *might*, *may* and *could* sometimes do.
Go through the examples with the class and then have
them complete the sentences in ways that are true for
them. They can then share their answers in pairs or
small groups.

2 | Discuss

The statements here show students how useful *tend to*
can be. It would sound odd if someone said *Men eat
more junk food than women*, but by adding *tend to* it
sounds more acceptable and less of an over-
generalisation. First have students discuss the five
statements in pairs. Then divide the class into all-male
and all-female groups. Allow students time to come up
with *tend to* statements about the differences between
men and women before getting them in male/female
pairs to compare their ideas. You could extend this
activity by having students write on other topics, using
tend to to be more cautious. Possible topics include their
impressions of the British/Americans/Australians etc.,
descriptions of people from their own country, the food
in their country compared to food in another country
they know, etc.

11 Telling stories

Unit overview

General topic
Anecdotes and stories.

Dialogue
Diane tells Cathy about the time her father didn't recognise her.

Reading
A woman has a spider living in her ear.

Language input

- Vocabulary to describe hairstyles: *He's got spiky hair, She's got dyed red hair,* etc.
- Slang expressions: *pinch my wallet, chuck it to me,* etc.
- Storytelling expressions: *Really? So, … , Well, … , Did I ever tell you about the time I … ,* etc.
- -ing clauses: *I was just standing there, minding my own business, The car broke down going up the hill.*
- Idiomatic language to make comparisons and exaggerate: *drive like a lunatic, I'm dying for a coffee,* etc.

Language strip

Have students choose any expressions they find interesting and, on their own, find out more about them. In a later class, ask them to share the information. For a small group activity, ask them to sort the expressions into any of the following categories: those that are said by the teller of the story (e.g. *So, to cut a long story short*), those that are said by the listener (e.g. *Really?*), those that could start a story (e.g. *You'll never believe what happened to me this morning*), and those that could be a response at the end of a story (e.g. *I don't believe a word of what you're saying*). Remind students to record any expressions they see themselves using in their notebooks. You might need to explain some of the following expressions:

- You might say *Do you think I was born yesterday?!* to show that you know someone is telling you something untrue or is trying to trick you. For example:
  A: *The ring? Well, I used to be married. I just can't be bothered to take it off.*
  B: *Oh, come on. Do you think I was born yesterday?!*

- You might say *Now I've heard everything!* in response to a very unusual story. For example:
  A: *… and it turned out that taxi driver was none other than Bruce Willis. Apparently, he likes to do it in his spare time.*
  B: *Now I've heard everything!*

- You say *So, to cut a long story short* to leave out a large part of your story in order to get to the main point. For example: *So, to cut a long story short, he asked me to marry him.*

- You would say *And if you believe that, you'll believe anything* after telling or hearing a story, true or untrue, that is very hard to believe. For example:
  A: *He said that he was really sorry he didn't show up at the restaurant. Something turned up at the last minute at work.*
  B: *And if you believe that, you'll believe anything.*

Lead in

Probably the best way to lead in to a unit on storytelling is to tell a story yourself. Students like to hear about personalised things from their teachers. After all, you are asking them to talk about themselves all the time! Tell the story in a natural way and have them ask you questions. Ideas could include when you met someone famous, the (un)luckiest day of your life, the funniest thing that has ever happened to you; the possibilities are endless. You could even tell a quick story at the start of each class session while working through this unit. You could start these stories by saying *Did I ever tell you about the time … ?*

Listening

1 Before you listen

Here is another opportunity for you to tell the class of any personal experiences before they do so themselves. If you don't have a story, make one up. Here is an example:
I was sitting in this small little restaurant in a tiny little village in the middle of the mountains of the northern Philippines, and this man comes up to me and says, 'Hello (Jim). What on earth are you doing here?' So I tell him, and we start chatting and all the time I'm thinking, 'Who is this guy?' Anyway, after about twenty minutes, I eventually realise he used to be my best friend at school.

2 While you listen (Hair today, gone tomorrow!)

Explain the situation. If there is no underground system in your area, find out if students have ever travelled on one. If not, explain a little about *changing trains* at stations and how the trains are divided into *carriages*. Also, refer students to the **Real English** note on *pinch*. Before playing the recording, see if anyone can explain the pun in the title – it's based on the idiom *Here today, gone tomorrow*, which means things come and go quickly. Explain that students should listen and then answer the two questions. Make sure they cover the text while they are listening. They can then discuss their answers in pairs.

Answers

1. It happened sometime last year/about a year and a half ago, on the underground.

2. Diane's father didn't recognise her to begin with, but in the end she spoke to him and he finally recognised her.

Let students read the conversation as you play the recording again. Then ask them to fill in the first two or three gaps from memory, in pairs, before playing the recording with pauses so that they can check and fill in the missing words. Do this two or three gaps at a time until the end. Play the recording through one more time with students following the text. If you want them to read the conversation, or parts of it, in pairs, use the tapescript on page 152.

As a quick follow-up, you could ask students to find examples of *get* expressions in the conversation to add to their notebooks (e.g. *I decided to get all my hair cut off, get his train back to Durham*).

3 Speaking

The questions here lead on from the conversation and give students a chance to talk about their own ideas and experiences in small groups. Make sure that they know what *ignore* means by asking them to complete this definition:
If you ignore someone, you refuse to … .
Possible ways to complete the definition are *acknowledge, pay attention to, speak to them.*

To help with the first question, you might need to give students some examples first:
Would you ignore someone you know on a bus if they were with someone you really couldn't stand?

How about if you saw a friend having dinner with someone other than their partner?

For the second question, after students listen to all the group members' stories, they choose the best one and tell it to the whole class.

Using vocabulary

1 Hairstyles

Lead in to this exercise by asking whether anyone has radically changed their hairstyle like Diane or by telling the class a personal story. Explain that some hairstyles are represented by more than one picture. Once students have matched the descriptions to the pictures, you could ask them to rank each person's hairstyle from 1 (favourite) to 8 (least favourite), and to explain their choices in pairs. Write a few expressions on the board to help:
I quite like this one.
I wouldn't be seen dead with hair like that.
I like it, but it wouldn't suit me.
I wish I could do that with my hair.

Alternatively, students could suggest which hairstyles would suit other members of the class or you! For vocabulary building, elicit or give some typical collocations for *hair*: *dye your hair purple, bleach your hair, cut off all your hair, lose your hair,* or other expressions to talk about hairstyles: *have a perm, have highlights.* Follow up with the small group discussion questions at the end of the exercise.

Answers

1. (spiky hair) – picture C
2. (curly hair) – picture B
3. (fringe) – pictures E and G
4. (dreadlocks) – picture A
5. (dyed red hair) – pictures B and G
6. (pigtails) – picture E
7. (hair extensions) – pictures D and H
8. (short back and sides) – pictures C and F

Review this vocabulary at a later time by having the class cover the list of expressions and then asking individual students to tell you the hair expression(s) when you call out the photograph number.

2 Slang

Ask students if they remember what *pinch his wallet* means and then explain that they are going to see some other slang expressions. Stress that it is good to know what these expressions mean as they are likely to hear them in everyday spoken English. However, they should be careful about actually using slang because of nuances of meaning and appropriacy for a particular situation. Illustrate this by asking whether it would be appropriate for a business executive to announce that she's decided to *flog the company*. Encourage them to check with their teacher first before using slang expressions. While checking the answers, ask further questions like: *What are other things you can chuck?*

There are more extended questions in **3 Speaking**.

Answers

1. c.   2. f.   3. e.   4. b.   5. d.   6. g.   7. h.   8. a.

3 Speaking

The task here uses a couple of the slang expressions to give students a chance to talk and tell stories. Lead in by telling the class of any personal experiences before having them tell each other in small groups.

4 Different kinds of stories

In this exercise, students work on several expressions with *story*. Although the focus is on types of story, you could lead in by asking for a few verbs collocations:
tell/listen to/believe + a story
the story + opens/begins/ends/is set in

You might want to explain that *the same old story* is a fixed expression said in response to hearing about something, usually bad, that happens regularly.

Answers

1. love 2. hard-luck 3. old 4. bedtime 5. inside 6. tall

5 Speaking

If you would like to develop this exercise into a more extended speaking practice, have students actually tell each other the stories. You may want to include folk/fairy stories as well. Again, tell the class a story yourself either before or after.

6 Storytelling expressions

This exercise presents examples of phrases called 'discourse markers' commonly found in storytelling conversations. These discourse markers help the flow of the conversation by, among other things, introducing, connecting and responding to events, as well as encouraging both the teller and the listener to keep on telling and listening.

Let students fill in the gaps individually and compare answers with a partner. Then play the dialogue twice to allow them to check their answers and to hear how the discourse markers sound, in particular the intonation pattern. Play the dialogue again, but this time pause after each discourse marker and let students practise saying the markers. Play the recording once more all the way through before students read the conversation in pairs.

Answers

1. Go on 2. Well 3. Really 4. so 5. Anyway
6. You're joking

7 Telling a story

This time the focus is on longer expressions. Go through the expressions, letting students hear them, and check that they understand their functions. Give students time to practise saying the expressions. Then focus their attention on the pictures. Ask a few questions to check that students know what the pictures are showing before getting them to prepare their stories in note form in pairs. Go around helping with vocabulary including collocations and longer phrases.

Once students have prepared their stories, have each student find another partner and tell their stories. Encourage the listener to use discourse markers like *Really? Go on, You're joking!* When they have finished, they find a new partner and tell the stories again. Explain that we get better when we do the same thing again and again; telling personal stories is a good example.

Using grammar

1 -ing clauses

Students have already come across -ing forms used as noun subjects (e.g. *Mountaineering can be pretty dangerous*) and after certain verbs (e.g. *I go skiing whenever I can, I've just finished reading it*). In this exercise the -ing form is used as a part of a clause. In traditional grammars, these are sometimes called 'present participle clauses', and are a common structure found in storytelling. These -ing clauses connect ideas without using a conjunction like *and* or *while*. To show this, write these examples on the board:
I was standing there and I was minding my own business.
I had a brilliant idea while I was coming to school today.

Then rub out the conjunctions (*and, while*), the repeated subjects (*I*) and the auxiliaries (*was*). Students can then do the exercise themselves, crossing out the repeated subjects and auxiliaries.

> **Answers**
>
> The unnecessary words are:
> 1. He was 2. They were 3. It was 4. He was 5. I was
> 6. They were 7. She was 8. We were 9. They were
>
> The missing parts of the sentences are:
> 10. minding my own business
> 11. passing through London on the underground
> 12. thinking, 'Who's this lunatic staring at me?'

2 Practice

This exercise gives students practice making their own -ing clauses. You could do the first sentences as an example, with the whole class making suggestions. Note that adding more than three -ing clauses is unusual. Students can work on this exercise in pairs before telling their favourite ones to the whole class.

> **Answers**
>
> Possible answers:
> 1. (There was this really strange-looking guy,) hanging around, talking to himself …
> 2. (I was rushing around madly,) trying to pack my stuff, hoping I hadn't forgotten anything …
> 3. (On Thursday I was driving along,) listening to the radio, singing along to this song …
> 4. (So there we were, in this fancy restaurant,) looking at the menu, trying to decide what to choose …
> 5. (My uncle was sitting there in the bar,) drinking double whiskies, smoking like a chimney …
> 6. (There was this huge crowd outside the parliament building,) waving placards (and) shouting slogans …

3 Pronunciation

Separate bits of information are usually clearly identified for the listener by pauses. When students fail to hear the pauses, comprehension can be difficult. Similarly, when students are speaking, if they pause too much or in the wrong places, they are more difficult to understand. Students need to learn where to pause and where not to pause. This is especially true when dealing with complex sentences containing many connected clauses such as those in **2 Practice**. **3 Pronunciation** focuses on correct pausing and stress in this kind of structure.

Tell the students to listen to the example and to mark the pauses with a slash (/). Play the recording again and ask them to underline the stressed syllables. After checking that everyone agrees, play sentences 1–5 first so that students can mark the pauses, and then a second time so that they can mark the stress. Remind students that stressed syllables are longer, higher and clearer than unstressed ones. Finish by having pairs read these sentences and those in **1 -ing clauses** to each other.

> **Answers**
>
> 1. There was this great big <u>dog</u>, <u>sitting</u> there, / <u>barking</u> at me.
> 2. It was five or six o'<u>clock</u> / and I was just <u>standing</u> there, / <u>minding</u> my own <u>business</u>.
> 3. My <u>dad</u> was actually coming <u>back</u> from a <u>business</u> trip <u>abroad</u>, / <u>passing</u> through <u>London</u>.
> 4. He keeps on <u>glancing</u> at me, <u>thinking</u>, / 'Who's this <u>lunatic</u> <u>staring</u> at me?'
> 5. I was <u>dancing</u> about in the <u>street</u>, / <u>acting</u> like a <u>fool</u>.
> 6. I was <u>lying</u> there on the <u>ground</u>, / <u>screaming</u> in <u>pain</u>.

4 Speaking

This exercise lets students retell their stories from **7 Telling a story** on page 78, this time trying to use -ing clauses. Again remind them that retelling helps them improve, especially in fluency. Tell students to read the **Grammar commentary, G17 Present participles** on page 163 to review the -ing clause structure.

Reading

1 Before you read

Ask the class if they have ever heard of anyone putting an animal in a microwave or finding a mouse in a pie. It's likely that someone in the class will have heard of a 'friend of a friend' who has had a similar experience. Get this student to tell their story and see if the rest of the class believes them. Remind students about *tall stories* and maybe talk about urban myths.

2 While you read (Spider woman)

Let students read the text. You could read it aloud or play the recorded version while they follow in their Coursebooks. Then have them share their reactions about whether they believe the story or not.

3 Speaking

This exercise again gives students an opportunity to tell stories. Make sure they know the animals and insects in the questions and then get them to talk in pairs. Point out that they would typically answer these questions with the contracted form *I'd*. Afterwards, select individuals to give answers to the class. For example:

A: *Marie, what would you do if you found a mouse in your bedroom?*
B: *I'd scream.*
A: *Why are you so scared of mice? They're harmless.*
B: *Well, …*

If any of these things has ever happened to someone, get them to tell their stories.

Using vocabulary

1 Idiomatic language

The use of idiomatic language is very common in storytelling. Although students may not feel they could use it themselves, they will undoubtedly come across it when listening to natural spoken English. Encourage them to translate and record in their notebooks those expressions that they like.

2 Idiomatic comparisons

To lead into this task, tell students that a friend of yours has just bought a new bike. Elicit from the class what aspects of the bike your friend might be pleased about and want to emphasise (speed, size, attractiveness, etc.) Next, ask what objects are known for these qualities (rockets, elephants, models). Then explain that if we want to emphasise some quality, we often make a comparison using *like*, but often the comparison is rather an unusual one. Now show them the two examples. Ask them to guess what is so good about the bike (it is fast) and speculate on why a horse might be known for having a big appetite.

Students can then work on the sentences 1–8 in pairs. As you check their answers, ask what quality is being emphasised and give the class practice saying the expressions. Pairs can then test each other: one person reads the first part of sentences 1–8, and their partner completes the expression without looking at the Coursebook.

Answers

1. (drank) like a fish (= drank a lot)
2. (was driving) like a lunatic (= was driving badly/erratically)
3. (treats her) like dirt (= treats her badly)
4. (looked) like death warmed up (= looked terrible)
5. (smoke) like a chimney (= smoke a lot)
6. (runs) like clockwork (= runs efficiently/regularly)
7. (slept) like a log (= slept well/deeply)
8. (get on) like a house on fire (= get on well)

Get students to guess what the three expressions at the end of the exercise mean:

- If you've *got a memory like a sieve*, you've got a very bad memory and forget things all the time. You might need to draw a sieve to give students a hint. For example: *Oh I forgot that I was going to give you a test today. Memory like a sieve!*
- If you *feel like a fish out of water* in a particular social situation, you feel very uncomfortable and out of place.
- If you *spend money like water*, you spend a lot of it – quickly, and probably more than you can really afford to!

Finish up by getting small groups to discuss the questions at the end. You may want to add questions like:

Does the public transport system in your city run like clockwork?

Do you know anyone who spends money like water/drinks like a fish/drives like a lunatic?

3 | Exaggerating using idioms

This is another way of emphasising by using idiomatic language. Have the class tell you what they think Diane means (she thought he would be really shocked), and then explain how death and illness are often used in idiomatic expressions. You can refer back to the expression *like death warmed up* to make the connection with the previous exercise (**2 Idiomatic comparisons**). Students can then work through the sentences in pairs. Knowing what part of speech is missing can help if they are having trouble. Having completed this part, they should then discuss what each sentence means and add the expression to one of the sentences a–i. While checking the answers, practise the stress and intonation patterns.

Answers

1. dying (I'd really like a coffee.)
2. murder (She's allowed to do all kinds of things that other people are not allowed to do.)
3. killing (My feet really hurt.)
4. murder (It's very difficult trying to get him to do things.)
5. died (I was very surprised/shocked/pleased when he told me that!)
6. died (I laughed a lot.)
7. death (I'm really fed up with it.)
8. die (I'd be really hurt/upset if anyone else found out.)
9. kill (If he does it again, I'll be really annoyed/I'll get really angry with him.)

a. 7. b. 3. c. 1. d. 6. e. 5. f. 8. g. 2. h. 4.
i. 9.

Finish off by discussing how these expressions might be translated into students' own languages and whether they have other idiomatic expressions involving death.

Wrap up

You can end this unit by asking the class to retell one of the many stories they have heard, from you or other students, while working through this unit. Give them the sentence starter *I heard this really funny/strange/sad/ disgusting story the other day* and have them tell another student. Alternatively, have them write the story for homework.

Unit overview

General topic
Amazing stories and urban myths.

Reading
- The things children get up to when they are left alone.
- Urban myths.

Language input
- Past continuous and -ing clauses to comment on incredible stories: *What was the kid thinking of, spending all that money?*
- Past continuous and past simple: *It was raining really heavily as I was leaving, so I grabbed an umbrella.*
- On the way: *We stopped off and had something to eat on the way to the match.*
- Travel words: *He's away on a business trip, There's a coach tour of the city, I always try and travel light*, etc.
- Vague language: *about thirty or forty people, There were no drinks or anything like that, He's about forty-ish*, etc.

Language strip

Have students choose any expressions they find interesting and, on their own, find out more about them. In a later class, ask them to share the information. For a small group activity, ask them to find those expressions that could be used by the teller of a story (e.g. *You should've seen the mess it made*) and those that could be used by the listener (e.g. *What a funny story*). Alternatively, they could find expressions containing modal auxiliaries (*Boys will be boys! That couldn't happen here*). You might need to explain some of the following expressions:

- If someone *gets away with something*, they are not caught or discovered doing something bad. For example: *He thought he'd got away with it until the police knocked on the door.*
- If something is *weird*, it is strange. For example: *It was kind of weird seeing my younger brother dressed up in a suit.*
- If you say something *beats them all*, you mean it is the best. For example: *I've had a lot of cars in my lifetime, but this one beats them all.*
- You use *That couldn't happen here* to say that you think such a thing would never happen in your country/city/home. For example: *Children openly buying drugs on the street? That could never happen here!*

- You say *Boys will be boys* to excuse any rough, noisy or naughty behaviour by a particular boy or group of boys because you think it is normal for boys to act that way. For example:
  A: *Bobby's got into trouble for fighting at school.*
  B: *Well, boys will be boys.*
- You would ask *Not the (famous name)?* in response to someone telling you that they met someone called (famous name) to check whether they actually met the famous person or just someone with the same name. For example:
  A: *You'll never guess who I saw in the pub last night – Kylie Minogue.*
  B: *What? Not, the Kylie Minogue?*
  A: *No, Aiden Minogue's little sister.*

Encourage students to record in their notebooks any of these expressions they feel might be useful, along with an appropriate translation.

Lead in

Use the photograph at the bottom of the page to start the unit. Ask students where this photo was taken and what these boys (lads) might have been up to. You might want to teach *just hanging out at the shopping centre*. Ask the class if anyone can work out where they've just been. Then ask further questions like:
What sort of things did you get up to with your friends when you were that age?
Do/Did you ever get into any trouble?

This leads in nicely to the first task.

Reading

1 He used to be so nice!

Explain that initially students should work with a partner, adding three more things to the list, and then on their own decide on the most and least serious. Then they explain their choices to their partner. Before students talk about whether they ever did any of these things, write some useful language on the board:
I only did it once.

I used to … all the time.

I never used to … , but I knew the boy/girl who did. (In this context, *I never used to* is more common than *I didn't use to*.)

(For a definition of *Boys will be boys*, see the notes for the **Language strip.**)

2 Collocations

This pre-reading activity contains collocations from the reading text on page 83 (**Home alone**). Have students work in pairs and then ask them further questions while checking the answers. For example:

Where do you find cigarette burns?

If you're grounded for a week, are you allowed to go out with your friends? How about to school?

Are adults ever grounded?

If you won £1 million, would you immediately go out on a spending spree?

Have students add these collocations to their notebooks.

> **Answers**
>
> 1. g.   2. e.   3. a.   4. c.   5. h.   6. b.   7. d.   8. f.

3 Before you read

Explain the general theme of the article and have pairs of students predict what the stories might be about, basing their predictions on the title and the collocations in **2 Collocations**.

4 While you read (Home alone)

Have students read the text to see if any of their predictions were right and then discuss their reactions in pairs. Write some sentence starters on the board to help:

I didn't believe the one about …

I wasn't surprised by the story about …

The best story was the one about …

Encourage students to go back and underline or ask about any interesting expressions or surprising collocations.

5 I can't believe it!

This exercise introduces students to a pragmatic use of the past continuous that is rarely mentioned in traditional grammars. Have students read the three examples and then choose the matching response.

> **Answers**
>
> 1. b./f.   2. a./e.   3. c./d.

Now students can practise, asking and responding in pairs. Explain that in the responses, the function of the modal auxiliary is either to speculate on something (*must be, could have been*) or to comment on how the situation could have been avoided (*should have*). Write the patterns on the board for students to copy in their notebooks:

A: *What were/was … doing, … -ing? / What were/was … thinking (of), … -ing?*

B: *I know! He/she/they should/shouldn't have … / I know! He/she/they could have/must …*

After writing their own sentences based on the article, students can again practise asking and responding in pairs.

> **Answers**
>
> Possible answers:
>
> A: What was the writer thinking of, covering up the cigarette burns with bits of carpet.
> B: I know. He should have just admitted it straight away.
>
> A: What were Terry and Jerry doing, setting off fireworks indoors.
> B: I know. They must be mad.
>
> A: What was John Thomas thinking of, shooting a gun like that.
> B: I know. He could have killed someone.
>
> A: What were his parents thinking of, keeping a gun in the kitchen cupboard.
> B: I know. They should have kept it locked away.

Using grammar

1 Past simple and past continuous

These two tenses are commonly used in telling stories. The past continuous is often used to set the scene of a story – actions occurring over an extended period of time, while the past simple is used for the main events – single, completed actions. In this exercise the past simple/past continuous distinction is implicitly introduced. The context helps students initially to match the two halves of the sentences, and only once they have to underline the verb forms at the end is the focus on tense made more explicit.

Answers

1. d.   2. a.   3. b.   4. c.   5. h.   6. g.   7. e.   8. f.

The past tense verb forms are:

1. was just sitting, started
2. was leaving, remembered
3. was raining, was leaving, grabbed
4. was living, were happening
5. was just going, rang, was going
6. went, came
7. were trying, won
8. resigned, found

2 Grammar discussion

Here you are helping students develop guidelines for how the two tenses are used. Ask them to individually choose the 'wrong' sentence in each group of three and then to discuss their choices with a partner, also explaining the differences between the two that are correct. When they have finished, ask them to work together as a class on a guideline to explain the use of the two tenses and write it on the board. Modify it in any way necessary, adding a time diagram if you wish, and then go through the answers.

Answers

The wrong sentences are:

1a. Finding a single diamond does not happen over a period of time.

2b. Getting stopped by the police does not happen over a period of time.

3b. Coming home on the tube should be expressed as a continuous action, happening over an extended period of time, as it is the background to seeing the old friend.

The differences between the two correct sentences are:

In 1b. the speaker suggests that the problems were being found over a period of time, while in 1c. there is no suggestion of a period of time. Perhaps the problems were found on one occasion.

In 2a. *got stopped* is seen as one completed action. In 2c. *getting tired* is expressed as happening over a period of time.

In 3a. *I was coming home* expresses that the journey was in progress and a background event. In 3c. *I came home on the tube* is seen as a single action caused by missing the bus.

Once students have finished this exercise, tell them to first read, or reread, the **Grammar introduction, Grammar: the verb** on page 157 for consolidation of their understanding of simple and continuous forms, and then read the **Grammar commentary, G18 Past simple and past continuous** on page 163.

3 Grammar check

This exercise provides further practice on the two verb forms and could be done either in class or for homework. Point out useful collocations and phrasal verbs while going through the answers (*my car broke down, bumped into an old friend, tidying my room up, turned up on my doorstep, came rushing into the room, boiling up some water*). Encourage students to add those they think they might need to their notebooks.

Answers

1. broke down   2. was walking   3. saw   4. were walking
5. was thinking   6. came   7. found out   8. was boiling

The question at the end of the exercise (*What were you doing when the clock struck twelve on 31st December 1999?*) shows how the past continuous can be used to express what was in progress at a particular time in the past. For this task, you could ask students to create a list with all the names of their classmates. Students can then mingle and find out what each person in the class was doing at the end of the last century and write it down on the list next to the person's name. Check students are using the past continuous form in their answers. You can extend this activity further by asking students to think of another significant event and ask:
What were you doing on/when …

Using vocabulary

1 On the way

This is a common expression used when giving the background to a story. Write the pattern on the board so students can write it in their notebooks, and tell them to record a few examples from this exercise. There are also some useful expressions with *get, go, take* and *have*, for example, *got car sick, went straight into the back of him, took a wrong turn, had a look around*, that they can record.

Answers

1. broke down
2. took a wrong turn
3. got a puncture
4. stopped off
5. had an accident
6. got lost
7. got car sick
8. bumped into
9. a pile-up
10. almost had an accident

2 Speaking

Use the questions here to practise the language from
1 **On the way**. Allow a few minutes preparation time
before having students wander around telling a few
people their stories. Remind them that the past
continuous is common for setting the scene of a story.

3 *Trip, tour, travel, etc.*

Start off by writing the words *trip, tour, journey* on the
board and ask if anyone can explain the difference.
Allow students to make suggestions, but don't comment
on whether they are right or wrong. Then ask for
different collocations for the words. Write them on the
board too. For example:

a business trip
a guided tour
a long journey

Explain to students that knowing what collocations are
used (and *not* used) will help them understand the
difference between the words. Then have students
complete the task. As you are checking the answers, add
more collocations to the board.

Answers

1. flight 2. journey 3. travel 4. travelling 5. trip 6. trip
7. travel 8. travelling 9. trip 10. tour 11. journey
12. tour

4 Speaking

Introduce this speaking task by telling the class of a
personal experience or even a favourite travel story
first. Then have the class work in small groups.

5 Being vague

Introduce this exercise by asking the class some
questions:
How old am I?
How long have I been teaching?
What was the first expression I taught you last week?

In this way you can show that often we don't have the
precise answer to a question. Explain that we also
sometimes don't want to be precise. Then explain that
students will learn some expressions that will allow
them to be less precise.

While going through the answers to 1–8, ask further
questions like:
What situation could they be describing?
What do you think the policeman said?
What could cost two hundred and something pounds?

Say the examples so that students can hear how these
expressions sound, especially the reductions in *sort of*
and *what's his name*. Point out the **Real English** note
for *sort of/kind of*.

Answers

1. b.   2. b.   3. b.   4. b.   5. b.   6. b.   7. a.   8. a.

6 ... or something / ... or anything

Here is another structure that allows us to be vague.
Have students read the examples and then ask them to
explain when to use *or something* and *or anything* (*or
something* is used with affirmative statements and
questions, *or anything* with negative statements and
questions). While you are checking the answers, ask
questions to generate connected language:
What else could you use to break into a car?
Have you ever flown on a budget airline?
Would you rather fly cheaply or comfortably?

Answers

1. a bit of wire or something
2. showers or anything
3. a hammer or something
4. or something like that
5. food or anything

7   *-ish*

Remind students that in the first unit (**1 Talking about people**) they came across *darkish hair* and that the ending *-ish* is another way to be less precise. As an extra exercise, students could describe some of the photos in this unit and elsewhere in the book using vague language. Get students to look at the picture on page 73 and ask:

Is the woman smiling? (Well, sort of smiling.)
What colour is her hair? (It's reddish.)
What colour is the man's hair? (It's sort of brown.)

Ask similar questions about the people with the different hairstyles on page 77.

> **Answers**
>
> 1. sixty-ish 2. yellow-ish 3. seven-ish 4. purple-ish
> 5. long-ish 6. tall-ish

Reading

1   While you read (Urban myths)

Explain to the class that they are going to read four stories, one of which is true and three of which are urban myths. Explain that an urban myth is a story that a lot of people have heard and think is true, but actually isn't. Divide the class into four groups and select one story for each group to read and try to remember so they can re-tell it later. Students should use dictionaries for unfamiliar vocabulary. Then form new groups of four.

Students re-tell their stories to others in their new group without the help of the Coursebook. After everyone has told their story, let students discuss which one is true. As an alternative, read the four stories aloud to the class or play the recorded versions. After this, students can discuss as a class or in small groups if they think they really happened or not.

> **Answers**
>
> *Sunk by a flying cow* is definitely true!

The title *What a rat!* is playing with words. The story is about a water rat, but the expression *What a rat!* means *What a dishonest, disloyal person!* Playing with words is common in British newspaper headlines. Ask the students if it is common in their language.

2   Speaking

If students have Internet access, ask them to search for more urban myths on the web. Ask them to bring any stories they think are interesting to class to put on the wall or notice board for others to read, or ask them to re-tell their story to the class or to a small group.

Review: Units 9-12

The exercises here can be used as a quiz. **5 Look back and check: Linking ideas**, however, is better done as a discussion in pairs.

1 | Tenses

Answers

1. must've been 2. I broke 3. I left 4. came up, started 5. I was cooking, I didn't answer
6. I was watching, went 7. Were you living, died
8. I didn't arrive

2 | Multiple choice

Answers

1. b. 2. b. 3. a. 4. b. 5. b. 6. b. 7. a. 8. b.
9. a. 10. b.

3 | Tend to

Answers

1. I tend not to eat sweet things.
2. I tend not to go out much during the week.
3. I tend not to drink.
4. I tend to take the bus to work.
5. People in my country tend to be quite religious.
6. People in my country tend not to invite friends round to their houses.
7. People in my country tend to spend their holidays with their families.
8. Women tend not to smoke much in public.

4 | Conversation

Answers

1. a. 2. j. 3. d. 4. c. 5. h. 6. f. 7. b. 8. e.
9. i. 10. g.

5 | Look back and check: Linking ideas

Answers will vary.

6 | Expressions

Answers

1. You went where
2. You can say that again
3. when all of a sudden
4. You must be mad
5. or something like that
6. sick to death of

7 | Collocations

Answers

1. c. 2. a. 3. i. 4. g. 5. h. 6. d. 7. b. 8. e.
9. j. 10. f. 11. q. 12. k. 13. l. 14. r. 15. m.
16. n. 17. o. 18. p.

8 | Real English

Answers

1. c. 2. d. 3. g. 4. a. 5. f. 6. e. 7. h. 8. b.

9 | Idioms

Answers

1. f. 2. a. 3. h. 4. g. 5. b. 6. e. 7. d. 8. c.

10 | What can you remember?

Answers will vary.

11 Vocabulary quiz

Answers

1. You would glare at them.
2. Possible answers: milk, money, petrol, time, food, paper
3. Someone who's able to make good decisions.
4. It could mean you're just going out for a drink or dinner with them, or that you're now boyfriend and girlfriend.
5. No! It just means that you accidentally meet them.
6. If he does something wrong but doesn't get punished for it. It does not mean that he actually killed someone.
7. Someone who's already divorced.
8. Will you marry me?
9. You get on well.
10. You might wear a wig if you're bald or want to try a new style.
11. You fall asleep.
12. You would do the washing.
13. No, they are attracted to you.
14. One that I found too personal!
15. A serial killer.
16. You surf the net.
17. They're young men.
18. Answers will vary: any film that is extremely popular and has made a lot of money is fine.
19. In the cloakroom.
20. You like them.

Learner advice: The authors speak!

Answers will vary.

Unit overview

General topic
Meeting people and catching up on news.

Dialogue
Barry and Sharon catch up with each other's news.

Reading
Four people want to get in touch with someone from their past.

Language input

- Expressions with get: *I really need to get some sleep, He never seems to get the message*, etc.
- Present perfect simple and present perfect continuous: *I've found your passport, I've been waiting for ages.*
- Present perfect adverbs and collocations: *I've just bumped into Harry on the tube, I've been studying for the past three years*, etc.
- Expressions with *point*: *I just don't see the point in complaining, It's still a very sore point with him*, etc.
- Using *I wish* + the past perfect for past regrets: *I wish I'd asked her for her address.*

Language strip

Have students choose any expressions they find interesting and, on their own, find out more about them. In a later class, ask them to share the information. For a small group activity, have students sort the expressions into the following groups: those used near the beginning of a conversation (e.g. *Don't you remember me?*), those used in the middle of the conversation (e.g. *I keep meaning to do that myself*) and those used near the end of the conversation (e.g. *Give my regards to Jill*).
You might need to explain some of the following expressions:

- You say *Oh, that reminds me* when something the other person said makes you remember something. For example:
  A: *I've just been shopping.*
  B: *Oh, that reminds me. I haven't got anything for dinner.*
- You can add a comment like *which was nice* after telling someone about something you have done. For example: *My husband and I went to Sydney for our last holiday, which was nice.*
- You say *I keep meaning to do that myself* about something you intend to do but haven't done yet. For example:
  A: *I've been going jogging every morning.*
  B: *Good for you. I keep meaning to do a bit myself.*

- *I'd better be going, Must dash!* and *It's been lovely seeing you* are used to end a conversation.
- You say *Give my regards to someone* when you want the person you are talking to say hello to another person for you.
- If you *lose touch with someone*, you are no longer in contact with them. You say *Keep in touch* when you want the other person to call you, write to you or visit you regularly.
- *We've got two now* probably refers to two children.

Remind students to add any expressions they could see themselves using to their notebooks.

Lead in

If possible tell the class about a personal story of bumping into an old friend. Alternatively, talk about one of your best friends now or when you were a child. Have the class ask you questions. Then ask them if they can recall any useful expressions that you used.

Listening

1 Eleven questions

Explain the task and make sure students understand the idea of a formal reunion of old friends. For older groups, ask if anyone has been to one. If so, ask them to describe what it was like. Did they like it? What sort of things did they talk about? Had people changed? Were there any major shocks?

Go through the expressions focusing on how they are said, in particular the intonation and stress. As they are usually said excitedly to a person that the speaker hasn't seen for a long time, they will be spoken with a relatively higher pitch and a wider intonation range than usual. You could demonstrate with the first expression, saying it in different ways and asking if it sounds appropriate for the context. Then have students practise saying the expressions themselves.

You might talk about possible responses to the first two expressions as a class before having students do the rest on their own. Note that although questions 2, 3 and 4 are not questions, they still anticipate some sort of response. While checking the answers, ask about other ways students might finish questions 9 and 10. For example:
Do you still go to church?
Are you still going out with John?
Are you still really into music?
Do you still live in London?
Do you still play in a band?

Once students have worked out responses to as many of these questions and comments as possible, get them to mingle as if they were at an actual reunion, asking questions and making comments to the people they come across.

2 I haven't seen you for ages

If you haven't already talked about these questions yourself, this would be a good opportunity to do so, as it provides the class with a good model for when they do it. Have students talk about these questions in pairs.

Photo opportunity

You could use the three photographs on page 92 to provide some more practice with conversations. Have pairs of students choose one of the photographs and write the opening dialogue. They can use expressions from **1 Eleven questions**, as well as the language strip. While they are working on this, move around checking their work and helping with vocabulary where necessary. Then let the students practise their dialogues before performing them for another pair or, if you wish, in front of the class.

3 While you listen (Long time, no see!)

Explain the setting and check that the class understands *bump into* by asking:
Did Sharon and Barry plan to meet in the street?

Check that students understand *are catching up with each other's news* by asking why we use *catch up* like this. Give them other examples of these expressions too:
I bumped into John the other day.
I need to catch up with what's going on back home.

Explain that the title *Long time, no see!* is a fixed expression and point out the **Real English** note on page 93. Go over the two questions and have students listen to the conversation with the text covered. They can then discuss the answers in pairs.

Answers

1. Barry's been working really long hours. He went to his grandmother's birthday party last weekend.

2. Sharon went to an art exhibition on Sunday, visited her friend Richard, did a bit of shopping at Camden market, and she's been doing things for college.

Then let students read the conversation as you play the recording again. Ask them to fill in the first two or three gaps from memory in pairs, before you play the recording with pauses so that they can check and fill in the missing words. Do this two or three gaps at a time until the end. Play the recording through one more time with students following the text. If you want students to read the conversation, or parts of it, in pairs, use the tapescript on page 153.

You might want to draw students' attention to the expressions *I went for a lovely meal/walk* and *I went and saw that exhibition.* You may need to explain that if something *causes a lot of fuss*, people have strong opinions about it, often negative. Point out the **Real English** note on *actually*. Go over the explanation and example, and then write the following sentences on the board asking students to write responses using *Well, actually … :*
That party last night sounded really boring.
I suppose his children were really well behaved.
What did you think of that book I gave you?
Is that English course you're doing any good?

Check their answers by choosing one student to read the first statement and another student to reply and so on.

4 Speaking

Before having small groups discuss these questions, explain that we can describe something as *controversial* if it causes a lot of public argument or disapproval. Give some relevant examples and collocations (e.g. *highly controversial, a controversial plan/decision/public figure*). Explain that *yuk* is said to indicate that you think something is disgusting or unpleasant.

5 Expressions with *get*

This exercise focuses on some more expressions with *get*. If students haven't done so already, encourage them to devote a section in their notebook to *get* expressions. While going through the answers, ask questions to check if students understand and to generate connected language:
Has anyone ever got an electric shock?
What does 'five years' refer to?
Do you think getting five years in prison is too little?
What kind of job does the person in number 4 have?
What do you think Claire does to give the impression she's bored?
What kind of things should you do if you 'have a life'?

Answers

1. a terrible shock
2. five years
3. a doctor
4. some sleep
5. the impression
6. a life
7. the message
8. to the top

Using grammar

1 Present perfect simple and present perfect continuous

You may need to remind students that the present perfect is typically used when the action is seen from the perspective of the time of speaking (now) and has some relevance to it. This exercise explores the distinction between the present perfect simple and the present perfect continuous. Generally the continuous form is used to refer to things that are temporary, unfinished or that happen over an extended period of time, whereas the simple form is used to refer to single completed actions.

Have students look at the two examples and discuss which one is more likely. Ask them to explain their choice. Explain the general difference between the continuous and simple forms and ask if they want to modify their decision. Finally explain that *I've been waiting here for an hour* is the better choice because the speaker wants to stress the extended nature of the waiting. The speaker might use the simple form to stress that they have given up waiting, i.e., waiting is seen as a completed action (e.g. *I've waited here for an hour and he's not shown up, so I'm going by myself*).

The next example checks that students understand that the present perfect continuous talks about an action extended over time. The correct answer is *I'm afraid I can't go. I've broken my arm*. Here the simple form is better because the action of breaking an arm happens only once – a single completed action. Ask students to tell you some other examples of actions that can't happen over an extended period of time. For example:
I've cut my finger.
I've fallen over.
I've won the Lottery.
I've passed my exam.

Now ask students to discuss the next set of examples. *You look as if you've been crying* is the correct answer in 1 because *crying* tends to be seen as occurring over an extended time. *I've found your passport* is correct in 2 because when you find something you have mislaid, it happens instantaneously – a single completed action.

Finally, it is important to note that it is not the meaning of the verb alone, but the whole context that decides whether the continuous form is used or not. *Find* can be used in the present perfect continuous in *We've been finding problems with the system all day* to emphasise the repeated nature of the action.

2 Adverbs with the present perfect

The examples here are all in the simple form and refer to single, completed actions. Although sometimes more than one answer is possible, the purpose of this exercise is to decide which form, the simple or continuous, is more probable. *Probable* language – language which students are likely to meet again – is more valuable than *possible* language from an acquisition point of view.

Answers

Probable answers:

1. never 2. just 3. almost 4. completely 5. almost
6. just 7. never 8. just 9. never 10. never

As an extension, you could ask students to work in pairs and create two-line dialogues based on sentences 2, 3, 4 and 6. For example:
A: *I've just bumped into Harry on the tube.*
B: *Really? How was he?*

3 Speaking

Have students complete the four sentence starters and then use them to start mini-conversations with a partner. Give them an example so they get the idea:
A: *I've just had a terrible thought.*
B: *What's that, then?*
A: *I think I've left the oven on.*
B: *I can give you a lift back to your house if you like.*

4 Present perfect collocations

Certain words co-occur in predictable ways, for example, *make a mistake*. It is also true that some words occur in particular grammatical patterns:
I haven't seen him for (time expression).
This exercise emphasises the way words and grammar co-occur in predictable ways. You needn't spend time explaining rules, just tell students to notice and remember the patterns. For example, you could explain that *the last three years* is a 'period of time', not a 'point in time', and is, therefore, used with *for* as traditional grammar books suggest. However, it is much more useful to teach expressions such as *for the past three years, since I was a child, for ages* as larger units, in the same way as you might teach *How are you?* Remind them that this exercise has some good examples for them to add to their notebooks.

Answers

1. a. 2. b. 3. b. 4. a. 5. a. 6. b. 7. b. 8. a.

Photo opportunity

Ask students to look at the two pictures at the bottom of page 94. Then have them generate endings, amusing or otherwise, to these sentence starters, using the pictures for ideas:

I've just seen something really funny, a …

I haven't … in ages

Sorry I'm late. I've been …

What's the matter? You look as if you've been …

What's the matter? You look as if you've just seen …

I've been studying to be a …

Have students share their ideas as a class or in small groups. (The picture on the left was taken in India; the picture on the right was taken at a market in Helsinki.)

5 Pronunciation

Here students practise some intonation patterns of how-questions followed by a present perfect comment. Play the recording and ask students how the speaker sounds – sad, excited, surprised, bored? This should elicit 'excited', so ask students why. Demonstrate the intonation pattern and then practise it. Then get students to practise saying 1–8 in pairs, after the recording.

6 Grammar practice

In pairs, students take turns asking and answering the questions in **5 Pronunciation**. Give them an example to get them started and encourage them to keep the conversations going. This is also good opportunity to practise the use of *Well, actually …* responses:

A: How are you? We haven't spoken for weeks.
B: Well, actually, I've been away for a couple of weeks.
A: Where have you been?
B: Helsinki, actually, working on a mushroom farm.

Using vocabulary

1 Expressions with *point*

Take this opportunity to remind students to notice and learn whole expressions and to make sure they transfer these expressions into their notebooks. Sometimes they can record expressions under two headings, as in the example *get to the point where you need …* . Explain that it is a good idea to record expressions in both places as it doubles the number of times they see it in their notebooks. Ask individual students to read whole

sentences back to you as a way of checking answers, and at the same time you can check their pronunciation and model the expressions for students to repeat after you.

Check that students understand the meaning of the expressions, and ask further questions to consolidate the language. For example:

Enrico, what would you say has been the high point in your life?

Claudia, do you think there is any point in learning grammar?

Carlos, you support Real Madrid, don't you? What do you think their strong points are? What about their weak points?

Answers

1. get 2. make 3. see 4. make 5. turning 6. strong
7. sore 8. high 9. there's no point 10. on the point of

2 Speaking

Use the questions here for small group discussion. Use the pictures to extend the discussion by prompting students to tell you of any similar experiences they may have had. Here are some examples of questions you could ask:

Do you know anyone who has just had a baby?

Do you know anyone who has just got married?

Reading

1 While you read (Long lost friends)

Read the information about the TV programme 'Surprise Surprise' and ask students to talk in pairs about whether this kind of programme is a good idea. Tell them that they are going to read about four people who would like to meet someone from their past. Students should then discuss with a partner which reunion story interests them most and why. They could also discuss which stories, if any, would not be a good idea to film.

2 Speaking

This task leads on from the reading text. Ask the class to think of someone from their past they would like to be reunited with and someone they would never like to see again. (If you wish, tell them about someone from your past.) Students can then talk about these people with a partner. Be sensitive to the fact, however, that this is very personal and could be uncomfortable for some people. Do not force students to talk about things they would prefer to keep to themselves.

3 | Idioms focus

The idiomatic expressions here are useful for talking about relationships. Students can work in pairs, sorting the expressions into two categories. Although they may not have met these expressions before, they could probably guess from the individual words whether the relationship is good or bad.

Answers

Describing a good relationship: 3, 4, 6
Describing a bad relationship: 1, 2, 5, 7

You may need to explain some of the following idioms:

- If you *get off on the wrong foot with someone*, your first meeting with that person does not go well; however, if you *hit it off with someone immediately*, it goes well.

- If you *have a bit of a soft spot for someone*, you like them or care about them.

- If you tell someone that *you'll be available if they need a shoulder to cry on*, you are saying that they can rely on you to comfort them if they are upset.

- If *there is no love lost between two people*, they don't like each other.

- If you *hate someone's guts*, it means that you strongly dislike the person.

While you're checking answers, ask students to think about any equivalents in their own language. Remind them to add the idioms they like, along with a translation, to their notebooks.

Have students memorise the idioms, and then, working in pairs, test each other. One person reads the examples a–g and the other completes the idiom without referring to the Coursebook. When they've finished, they can swap roles. Finish up by having small groups talk about the sentences at the end of the exercise.

Using grammar

1 | I wish

This exercise focuses on the use of *I wish* + the past perfect to express past regrets. We usually think of tenses as referring to time, such as the 'present' and the 'past'. However a past tense form can sometimes express 'a distance from reality', such as when we talk about hypothetical things. For example, we use the past simple in hypothetical conditional sentences about the present or future:
I wouldn't do that if I were you.

When we talk about hypothetical things in the past, we use a past perfect to express the further distance of the hypothetical action from the past reality:
If I hadn't been so lucky, I'm sure I would have been killed.

In a similar way, we use the past perfect to express what we wanted to happen. Have students read the example and then suggest their answers to you.

Answers

1. He regretted not asking her because he would like to get in touch with her.

2. We use the past perfect after *wish* to talk about past regrets.

Students can then work individually through the sentences 1–8, adding the correct forms before matching the follow-up comments a–h. Have them check their answers in pairs before listening to the recording to confirm.

Answers

1. 'd known
2. hadn't eaten
3. 'd travelled
4. 'd gone
5. hadn't wasted
6. hadn't spent
7. 'd met
8. hadn't lost

1. g.   2. h.   3. c.   4. d.   5. a.   6. e.   7. b.   8. f.

For the follow-up task ask students to complete the personalised sentence starters and then to explain them to a partner. Refer students to the **Grammar Commentary, G21 Wish** on page 164 and encourage them to record several examples of this structure in their notebooks.

2 | Role play

Here is a chance for students to use a lot of the language from the unit. Give pairs of students five or ten minutes to decide on the kind of things that could or would be said in their chosen reunion before trying the conversation together. One or two conversations could be performed for the class. For homework, ask students to write their own 'story' like the ones in this activity, explaining who they would like to meet again and why. Alternatively, ask them to write the conversation they imagine they would have once they are reunited with the old friend of their choice.

14 | Art

Unit overview

General topic
Describing works of art, talking about the purpose of art and recommending things you have seen.

Reading
Modern art.

Language input
- Expressions for recommending and not recommending: *You should go and see it, I'd give it a miss, if I were you,* etc.

- Vocabulary to describe paintings: *a portrait, a landscape, very detailed,* etc.

- Noun collocations with *cause: cause a riot, caused outrage,* etc.

- Relative clauses used to add a comment: *I went to that new Matisse exhibition, which was really nice.*

- Remembering expressions: *That reminds me, I keep meaning to see that myself,* etc.

Language strip

Have students choose any expressions they find interesting and, on their own, find out more about them. In a later class, ask them to share the information. For a small group activity, ask students to find expressions they might use when actually looking at a work of art (e.g. *What do you think of this one?*) and expressions you might use if you don't like it (e.g. *It's not really my cup of tea*). You might need to explain some of the following expressions:

- You would say *You call that art?* when you think it is not art and you don't particularly like it.

- If you say *He pickles sheep,* you are referring to the work of the contemporary British artist Damien Hirst, who has exhibited dead animals preserved in chemicals!

- If you *give something a miss,* you don't do it. For example:
  A: *Are you coming out with us on Friday?*
  B: *No, I've been really tired. I think I'll give it a miss this week and catch up with some sleep.*

- If someone is *arty,* they like things like the arts, drama, poetry, film, paintings, etc. However, it is sometimes used in a negative way to say that the person is pretentious.

Lead in

Write the word *art* on the board and ask the students what this word means for them. Ask further questions to get the discussion going. For example:
What things are generally considered 'art'?

What is an example of something that is generally considered 'art' but that you don't think is really art?

Would you describe a typical Hollywood blockbuster as 'art'?

Is a lesson a work of 'art'?

Using vocabulary

1 Speaking

Continue the discussion on 'art' by asking these questions to the class as a whole or have small groups discuss them. Finish off by having pairs discuss the two paintings and talking about their own artistic experiences. You might want do a little extra vocabulary work by eliciting some collocations for *exhibition*. For example:

go to an exhibition	*a photography exhibition*
see/attend an exhibition	*a sculpture exhibition*
have/hold an exhibition	*an exhibition of Italian/seventeenth century/modern art*

2 Recommending

This exercise introduces some useful phrases about going to exhibitions and making recommendations. You could lead into this exercise by asking why people often go to galleries when they are travelling, but never visit them in their own town or city.

First, ask students what they would say if they want to recommend an exhibition they have just seen to a friend. Then get them to put the first conversation in the correct order and to find an expression for recommending (*You should go and see it*). Play the recording so students can check their answers. Play the recording twice more, focusing on the stress and intonation patterns. Students can then practise the conversation in pairs, making sure they sound enthusiastic.

Note: The Hayward Gallery is in London.

Answers

Conversation 1: 1. a.   2. g.   3. f.   4. d.   5. c.   6. b.
                7. e.

Before listening to the second conversation, ask students what they would say if they didn't recommend seeing an exhibition. They can then put the conversation into the correct order and find the expression for not recommending (*I'd give it a miss if I were you*). Follow the same procedure as in the first conversation; however, this time remind students that they're not enthusiastic!

Note: The National Gallery is also in London.

Answers

Conversation 2: 1. a.   2. c.   3. b.   4. f.   5. d.   6. g.
               7. e.

3 Recommending expressions

This exercise introduces some more fixed expressions for making recommendations. Let students reorder the expressions in pairs and decide which are recommending and which aren't. Then play the recording so they can check their answers. Play the recording again, using it as a model for students to practise saying the expressions with appropriate stress and intonation.

Answers

1. It's OK if you're into that sort of thing.
2. It's a must.
3. I really recommend it.
4. I'd give it a miss if I were you.
5. It's well worth a visit.
6. It's not worth the entrance fee.
7. It's not really my cup of tea./It's not my cup of tea, really.

Numbers 2, 3, 5, are recommending; 1, 4, 6, 7 are not.

4 Practice

Get students to think of an exhibition, or some other event or place, they have been to recently, and whether they'd recommend it or not. In pairs, they should have a conversation using language from the previous exercises. They should begin like this:
I went and saw an exhibition (the Tower of London/a play called ... , etc.) at ... the other day/the other week.

5 Describing paintings

Here students work on vocabulary used to describe paintings. Once they've completed the sentences 1–8, have them check their answers in pairs. If you have any postcards of paintings, bring them in for students to describe using this vocabulary. Point out that *portrait*, *landscape* and *still life* are nouns and the other words are adjectives.

Answers

1. original 2. still life 3. portrait 4. detailed
5. landscape 6. traditional 7. colourful 8. abstract

As a class you could also add to the list of adjectives. Students may suggest adjectives that aren't typically used to describe paintings, so you can give them more appropriate ones. Here are some further examples: *ambiguous, avant-garde, boring, challenging, clichéd, decorative, dramatic, energetic, expressive, figurative, grotesque, intense, large-scale (small-scale), romantic, striking, subtle, symmetrical, vibrant, witty*

6 Speaking

If you've worked on some more adjectives in **5 Describing paintings**, students can use some of them to talk about their own favourite piece of art. If possible, tell the class about your favourite piece of art.

Reading

1 Before you read

Ask students if they like modern art and to give their reactions to the art shown in the picture on the right. You could also refer them to the language strip so that they can choose any of the expressions they feel might be appropriate.

2 While you read (Art Attack)

Ask students to read the article to find out the writer's opinion on modern art. Tell them not to worry about understanding every word and expression. When they have finished, they can share their ideas in pairs.

3 Speaking

Here students have the chance to reread the article, and interact with it by finding parts they agree with, disagree with and don't understand (the latter perhaps because of language). They can then use their marked-up text as the basis for a discussion with a partner. Go around helping with parts of the text that are still unclear. Encourage students to read the article again at home, adding any interesting expressions and collocations to their notebooks.

4 Collocations

We use the verb *cause* to introduce a result of something; this result tends to be negative. It is important to remind students that when we come across a word, we need to know a lot about it (its collocations, its typical patterns, its grammar, etc.). Have students look at the examples and see if they notice that all the nouns are negative in meaning. Pairs can then discuss what might have caused all these things. Choose a couple of good examples for each sentence and write them on the board so students can copy them into their notebooks.

You can have students talk about things in the news to make some *cause* sentences. Alternatively, you can bring in some newspapers and go through some recent events and decisions and have groups of students predict what the results might be. For example:
The decision to increase the tax on petrol will cause outrage among motorists.

If students want to express a result that is not negative, give them other verbs such as *lead to* and *result in*.

Using grammar

1 Relative clauses

This exercise concentrates on one use of a relative clause to add a comment. The two patterns are *which meant* ... and *which was* ... . Unlike other relative clauses that refer to a previous noun (e.g. *Don't you have a friend who can give you a lift?*), this type of relative clause refers to a previous statement. You can think of *which* as substituting for *this* or *it*. Give students a few minutes to think of, or write down their comments for 1–8 and then select a few students to give answers to the class, correcting where necessary. While going through the answers, make sure students hear how this pattern is said, in particular the pause and change in intonation at the comma.

Answers

Possible answers:

1. we stayed in the whole day
2. fascinating
3. really nice
4. a first for me
5. I was about an hour late
6. I had to wait another year before I could apply to go to university

2 Speaking

Write some sentence starters on the board to help:
I went and saw ...
I went for a ...
I was in ...

Give an example yourself, adding a comment with *which*, before having students tell each other in pairs. Note that if they want to use present perfect expressions, then the relative clause will probably be in the present:
They've just cancelled the last train, which means I need to call a cab.

Tell students to read the **Grammar commentary, G22 Relative clauses** on page 164 to review this structure.

Using vocabulary

1 Oh, that reminds me!

Go over the explanation at the beginning of the exercise. Then ask a student to read the example conversations with you; you yourself should read the part with the highlighted language. Make sure students hear the intonation patterns. Have them practise the expressions with you before getting them to read the conversations in pairs. Some students may put the stress on the first syllable of *myself*, so listen for that. They can then do the matching exercise in pairs before they listen to the recording to check their answers.

Answers

1. d.   2. c.   3. f.   4. e.   5. b.   6. a.

Although the conversations are full of useful expressions, the important ones for this exercise are

a. Oh, that reminds me. I must ...
b. I've been thinking about ... myself.
c. Oh, that reminds me. I must ...
d. I keep meaning to ... myself.
e. Oh, that reminds me. I must ...
f. Oh, I've been meaning to ...

2 Practice

This exercise consolidates the language from **1 Oh, that reminds me!** and provides a chance for freer practice. Initially, students add a third response to the conversations in **1 Oh, that reminds me!** They then develop their own conversations based on the prompts. Give them an example so that they can see how to do it:

A: *I must remember to buy a birthday card for my brother.*

B: *Oh, that reminds me, it's my dad's birthday next week and I still haven't got him a present.*

A: *How old is he?*

B: *I don't know exactly, late fifties or something.*

When students have finished, get each pair to choose one of their conversations to perform for another pair.

3 Speaking

This activity reinforces a lot of the language presented in this unit. First, have students read through the six examples, while you answer any questions they might have about the vocabulary. Then put them in small groups to discuss the questions. You might need to provide language. For example:

I think it's disgusting/outrageous/terrible/offensive.

It doesn't really worry/shock/annoy/bother me.

Point out to the students that street art is also known as graffiti. You could add questions like:

Is it wrong to paint on public property, even if it is artistic?

When is it OK? When is it not?

15 Describing things

Unit overview

General topic
Describing things.

Dialogue
Paul and Mick discuss films they have seen recently.

Language input
- Vocabulary to describe things: *horrendous, nothing special, terrific*, etc.
- Linked questions: *What's his house like? Is it big?*
- Conjunctions: *although, considering, in spite of*
- Negative questions: *Didn't you think it was really boring?*
- Idiomatic expressions to strengthen adjectives: *razor sharp, brand new*, etc.
- Comparing: *It was a bit like skiing, only a lot more difficult.*
- *Must* for guessing: *That must be nice, That must have been wonderful.*

Language strip

Have students choose any expressions they find interesting and, on their own, find out more about them. In a later class, ask them to share the information. For a small group activity, ask them to find expressions that express positive reactions (e.g. *Loved the food*) and negative reactions (e.g. *But the acting was horrendous*). You could also ask them to come up with a question or statement that prompts three expressions as a response. For example:
A: *What do you think of star fruit?*
B: *Star fruit? I've never eaten one.*

You could ask students to provide a response that answers three expressions that are questions. For example:
A: *Any good?*
B: *It's OK if you're into that sort of thing.*

You might need to explain some of the following expressions:
- If something is *horrendous*, it's very bad. For example: *The snow caused horrendous driving conditions in the north.*

- If you say *something or someone is not exactly something/someone famous* (e.g., Shakespeare, Superman), you are sarcastically saying that the former is nowhere near the standard of the latter. *To be or not to be* is a quotation from *Hamlet*.
- If you describe something as *a bit over-the-top*, you are criticising it for being excessive or extreme. For example: *The love scenes were a bit over-the-top, but it was generally OK.*
- If you describe food as *bland*, it doesn't have a lot of flavour. For example: *The food there can be a little bland, but it's certainly filling.*

Remind students to record any of the expressions that they like in their notebooks.

Lead in

You can lead in to the topic of describing things by telling the class about a place you've recently been to, a film, play or band you've seen, or a book you've read. Try to use a lot of descriptive adjectives. Let the students ask you a few questions about it. When you've finished, ask them to recall any of the adjectives you used and write them on the board along with their associated nouns. For example:
the acting – appalling

This leads in nicely to the first exercise.

Listening

1 Before you listen

Introduce this task by asking what the class thinks of a recent film and what adjectives they would use to describe it to a friend. Listen to their ideas and then explain that you are going to ask them to sort some adjectives for describing things into three categories: very good, not too good/mildly critical and very bad. Allow students to use their dictionaries and to compare their answers in pairs. Point out the **Real English** note for *over-the-top*. As you go through the list of adjectives in each category, ask students to listen for the stressed syllables and to underline them. Then have them practise saying the expressions in the phrase *It was (terrific/excellent etc.)*.

Answers

(with stressed syllables underlined)

Very good: ter<u>ri</u>fic, <u>ex</u>cellent, <u>won</u>derful, <u>mar</u>vellous, <u>bri</u>lliant, su<u>perb</u>

Mildly critical: a bit <u>bland</u>, very <u>or</u>dinary, nothing <u>spe</u>cial, on the <u>dull</u> side, a bit over-the -<u>top</u>, a bit disa<u>ppoi</u>nting

Very bad: <u>dread</u>ful, <u>hor</u>rible, ho<u>rren</u>dous, <u>dire</u>, <u>te</u>rrible, <u>aw</u>ful

2 While you listen

Play the recording of the three conversations and ask the students to write down the adjectives they hear. Ask them to note down what nouns are being described as well. Get students to compare answers in pairs before you play the recording for them one more time.

Answers

Conversation 1: fish – really nice: chicken – a bit bland; mushroom sauce – delicious (according to the waiter)

Conversation 2: wine – nothing special, very ordinary, a bit disappointing, not that bad

Conversation 3: the play *Macbeth* – brilliant, wonderful

While checking the answers you might ask whether any of the class would send back the wine or the chicken for being *bland* and *a bit disappointing*. Find out under what circumstances they would send food or wine back.

3 Practice

Students can work on these questions in small groups. You can use the two pictures at the bottom of the page to illustrate how the conversation might go:

A: *I was stuck in this traffic jam yesterday. It was horrendous. It took me five hours to get home.*
B: *Five hours? What a nightmare!*
A: *Apparently, there was a terrible accident on the motorway.*

A: *I went and saw one of those art films at the Duke of York's the other day.*
B: *What was it like?*
A: *A bit disappointing. To tell you the truth, I was more impressed with those legs sticking out of the roof.*
B: *Oh yeah, they're brilliant, aren't they?*

Go around monitoring the conversations and give any feedback on where adjectives may have been used inappropriately. For example, a journey would not normally be described as *bland*.

Note: The traffic jam in the picture is on a section of British motorway famous for delays. The legs on top of the cinema are on top of the Duke of York's cinema, a well-known landmark in Brighton.

4 Asking linked questions

This exercise focuses on how questions are often asked two at a time, particularly questions that ask for a description. The second question often presupposes the answer. For example, if you ask, *What's his house like? Is it big?*, you think it probably is big. Go through the two examples noting that *Any good?* instead of *Was it any good?* is an example of how ellipsis is commonly used in spoken English.

As there is a variety of possible answers, go around the class checking and correcting as the students are writing. Let students compare their finished answers with a partner before you play the recording. Play each suggested answer one by one, letting students repeat them, paying attention in particular to the stress and intonation patterns.

Answers

Probable answers:
2. What was that book like? Was it interesting?
3. What's your new job like? Are you enjoying it?
4. What was Tunisia like? Was it warm?
5. What's this CD like? Is it any good?
6. How was the match? Did you win?

5 Practice

So that students know what to do in this exercise, have them suggest questions for the first two situations, and then choose a couple of students to respond. For example:

A: *What was the weather like on your trip to Indonesia? Was it OK?*
B: *It was horrible. It rained every day.*

A: *What's your job like? Is it interesting?*
B: *It's OK, a bit on the dull side.*

Students can then ask each other in pairs.

Using grammar

1 Conjunctions

The conjunctions *although*, *considering* and *in spite of* often occur in conversations describing things. First, get students in pairs to talk about what each example means and to think about what kind of structure follows each conjunction. Students may not be able to articulate the exact differences in meaning, so read the **Grammar commentary, G23 Conjunctions** on page 164 together.

In this exercise, students can practise using the three conjunctions. Have them work individually before comparing answers with a partner. As you check their answers, ask them to explain why they chose the particular conjunction.

Answers

1. Talking about a new CD: a. considering   b. although
   c. although   d. considering
2. Talking about a trip: a. although   b. considering
   c. although   d. considering
3. Talking about buying a watch: a. although   b. in spite
   of   c. in spite of   d. although

3 Speaking

Before doing this exercise, have the class suggest a
couple of examples for you to write on the board.
You could also encourage linked questions as in
1 Conjunctions:

A: *So what's the food like at Chez George?*
B: *A bit disappointing, although I hear the steak's good.*

Listening

1 While you listen (Not exactly Shakespeare!)

Lead in by asking for the names of recent films and
asking questions like:
What was it like? Any good?
What did you think of it?

Explain the situation and ask students to listen for the
answers to the two questions. Make sure they cover the
text while they are listening for the first time. Have pairs
discuss their answers.

Answers

1. *Titanic* and *Bomb Alert 2*.
2. Paul really liked *Titanic*, Mick thought it was a bit
   over-the-top. Mick really liked *Bomb Alert 2*, Paul
   hasn't seen it – it's not his kind of thing.

Now see if students can fill in the first two or three
gaps from memory with a partner. Play the recording
again for students to fill in the missing words. Pause the
recording so they have time to write in what they hear.
Finally, play the recording again with students listening
while reading the tapescript on page 154. The missing
words are highlighted. Don't be afraid to ask students to
listen several times. The more students listen to natural
spoken English, the more chance they have of acquiring
that language and improving their performance.

Have students go back and find any adjective + noun
collocations they would like to remember. For example:
amazing special effects
wooden/brilliant acting
awful dialogue

Draw students' attention to the **Real English** note *It's
not exactly Shakespeare* and ask them to make similar
statements for these situations:

• Describing a cheap, run-down hotel: *It's not exactly the
  Hilton, is it?*

• Describing a battered old car: *It's not exactly a Rolls
  Royce, is it?*

• Describing someone who can't play tennis very well:
  She's not exactly Serena Williams, is she?

2 Speaking

This provides a follow-up for the listening activity.
Students should answer the questions in pairs and justify
their choices. Finish up by having the class nominate
their choices for the most over-the-top film before
having them vote. You could also extend this activity
with other categories: *most wooden acting, most amazing
special effects*, etc.

Using grammar

1 Negative questions

These kinds of questions can be confusing to students,
especially when it comes to answering them. Get
students to read through the introduction to the
exercise. Then ask them to change the following into a
negative question:
Do you want any of this pizza?
(Don't you want any of this pizza?)

Ask students to explain why someone might use the
negative rather than the positive question (The first
question is a kind of offer. The negative question
expresses surprise that the other person has not eaten
any of the pizza.) Ask how they would answer the
negative question (e.g. *No, I'm not that hungry/I do, but I'm
just waiting until I get my drink*). Students should then read
about the two patterns. Tell them to record these two
patterns along with a couple of examples from this
exercise in their notebooks. Play the recording, pointing
out the intonation pattern and then have students
practise the examples with a partner.

2 Grammar in context

Students can work through the short dialogues 1–8
individually. While you check their answers, ask further
questions. For example:
*Do you prefer watching films in English with subtitles or
without?*
Can you tell me about a film that was really slow?
What other adjectives could you use to describe a plot?
(simple/complicated)
Exactly how many Oscars did 'Titanic' win?
What kind of things are on late-night cable TV?

Answers

1. Don't you find (them hard to read?)
2. Didn't you think (she over-acted a bit?)
3. Didn't you think (it was a bit slow?)
4. Didn't you think (it was really romantic?)
5. Didn't you find (it quite funny, though?)
6. Didn't you find (him a bit too much like Robert De Niro?)
7. Don't you think (it's a bit over-rated?)
8. Didn't you think (it was just silly and typical of late-night cable TV?)

3 Grammar role play

Explain the task, checking that students understand what to do. Write some expressions on the board to help them think of how to express their ideas. For example:
Don't you find … ?
Don't you think … ?
I know what you mean.
Really?
Yes … , although …
It's a bit too … for me.

Give students three or four minutes to prepare and ask them to repeat the task at least once, perhaps with a different partner.

4 Idioms focus

This exercise focuses on idiomatic expressions that strengthen some adjectives. Encourage students to record these in their notebooks. Have them match the words first and then complete the sentences. While you check the answers, ask for other things that can be *razor sharp*, *dirt cheap*, *dead easy* and *rock hard*. Follow up by having pairs of students test each other: one person reading the words 1–8, the other trying to remember the adjective.

Answers

1. g. 2. a. 3. e. 4. h. 5. d. 6. b. 7. f. 8. c.

9. razor sharp 10. brand new 11. stark naked
12. wide awake 13. dirt cheap 14. fast asleep
15. dead easy 16. rock hard

5 Comparing

This exercise introduces students to a common way of using comparative structures in spoken English. Model the examples yourself, focusing on the pauses before *but* and *only*. Have students practise saying the examples after you, pausing in the appropriate places.

6 Describing things

Students can work on this matching exercise individually. While you check their answers, ask questions to generate other connected language. For example:
So, how would you describe food from your country?
Has anyone here been snowboarding? How was it?

Have students then practise the short dialogues in pairs.

Answers

1. e.   2. g.   3. b.   4. a.   5. f.   6. h.   7. d.   8. c.

7 Practice

Students can work in pairs describing the objects in the pictures. Write the sentence starter *It looks a bit like a … on the board to help them. For the second task, model a couple of examples first so students get an idea of how to write their descriptions. Ask them to guess what you're describing. For example:
It's a vegetable. It looks a bit like a carrot but it's white, with a much stronger taste. (a parsnip)

Have students work alone writing their sentences before they work with a partner for the guessing part. Refer students to the **Grammar commentary, G24 Comparing** on page 165 to review these structures.

8 *Must* for guessing

Introduce this section by telling the class about something bad that happened to you a while ago, for example, splitting up with your partner or finding your car stolen. Elicit some adjectives to describe the situation (e.g. *awful*, *terrible*) and write a couple on the board. Explain that one way to respond to this kind of story is to use an expression with *must have* and write an example using one the adjectives. For example:
That must've been awful.

Next, tell students about something you are looking forward to (e.g. a holiday, going away for the weekend). Again, elicit some adjectives to describe your feelings and choose one to show how you could respond in this situation. For example:
You must be really excited.

Explain that we use *must* to make a guess or draw a conclusion that we are pretty sure is true. We use *must've* to talk about the past and *must* to talk about the present/future. Let students read the two examples, then read the dialogues out loud so that they can hear the reduced pronunciation of *must be* and *must've*. Have them then practise saying the two dialogues in pairs. Tell them to review the **Grammar commentary, G25 Must for guessing** on page 165 after they've finished the exercise.

Students can work individually to complete the sentences 1–9 before comparing their answers with a partner. While you are checking the answers, ask questions to generate further connected language:

What's the opposite of a strong accent? (a slight one)

What do you do if the battery of a car is dead?

Has anyone been to Bali? What did you think of it?

What do you think the people in dialogue 8 are talking about?

Point out the **Real English** note on *doing over a hundred*. Ask students if they ever do more than eighty on the motorways.

Answers

1. must be 2. must be 3. must've been 4. must be
5. must be 6. must've been 7. must be 8. must be
9. must've been

---

9 Grammar in context

This exercise allows some freer practice in the use of *must* to make guesses. Students can work individually before getting together with a partner to practise giving their responses. Students will likely come up with a variety of answers; the ones below are just suggestions.

Answers

Possible answers:

1. That must be hard work.
2. That must've been nice/horrible.
3. That must keep you fit.
4. It must've been beautiful.
5. That must be awful.
6. That must've been horrendous.
7. It must've been awful.
8. That must be nice.

---

10 Practice

Read out the example, then tell students about something interesting you've done or seen recently and try and elicit a few replies using *must've been*. You might need to prompt this by writing *That must've been ...* on the board. Then give students some time to write down their own interesting experiences before they talk about them in pairs. Remind them that they can use a relative clause with *which* to add a comment, as in the example (*which was nice*).

Use the photographs at the bottom of the page to elicit the use of *must be* to draw conclusions about where the place is. Make sure students explain their choices. For example:

A: *The picture on the right must be somewhere in Northern Europe.*

B: *Why do you say that?*

A: *There are no trees!*

You can then ask students to draw conclusions about what it's like in those places. For example:
The place in the picture on the right must be quite windy. It must be quite tough living in the place in the picture on the left.

Note: The photos are, from left to right: the Orissa region in eastern India, Venice, Loch Seaforth in the Outer Hebrides.

To conclude this unit, you could have students write about a little-known place in their country for homework. Ask them to bring in their descriptions to class and to exchange them with another student. They then read their partner's writing and think of further questions to ask. Finally, they get together with their partner to talk more about the place they just read about.

Unit overview

General topic
Films, TV and censorship.

Reading
A film which was adapted for TV is criticised for not being violent enough.

Language input
- Vocabulary to describe films: *a kind of sci-fi thing, a costume drama, amazing special effects*, etc.
- Asking questions about films: *Who's in it? When was it made?* etc.
- Past perfect simple: *I'd never made a speech in my life before, He'd been married once before.*
- Vocabulary to describe groups of people: *audience, spectators, viewers*
- Television vocabulary: *remote control, channel, cable*, etc.
- Mixed conditionals: *If it hadn't been for her, I wouldn't be doing what I'm doing now.*

Language strip

Have students choose any expressions they find interesting and, on their own, find out more about them. In a later class, ask them to share the information. For a small group activity, ask students to find expressions that might be said when you're watching a film in a cinema (e.g. *Pass the popcorn*), those when you're watching TV (e.g. *Where's the remote control?*) and those which might be used in both situations. You could also ask them to come up with questions or statements that prompt some of the expressions as a response. For example:

A: *Anything good on tonight?*
B: *Sport, sport and more sport*

You could ask students to provide responses to some of the expressions that are questions:

A: *Who's in it?*
B: *Leonardo di Caprio.*

You might need to explain some of the following expressions:

- If you describe something as *rubbish*, you're saying it's not very good. For example:
  A: *What did you think of 'Halloween 13'?*
  B: *It was a load of rubbish! Even worse than 'Halloween 12'.*

- If you say *It's on cable*, it means that the programme is being shown on cable television.
- Some television stations *bleep out* words they think may offend people. You hear a sound instead of the word. The *f-word* is an alternative way of referring to the word *fuck*.

Remind students to record any of the expressions that they like in their notebooks.

Lead in

Lead in to this unit by asking questions like:
Did anyone see anything good on TV last night? What was it about?

Can anyone recommend a good film to see?

I feel like watching a video tonight. Anyone know of a good comedy?

Using vocabulary

1 What kind of film is it?

Begin by asking students about the films shown in the pictures on page 110. See if students recognise any of the actors.

Answers

The three films on page 110 are *Four Weddings and a Funeral, Titanic,* and *Braveheart.*

The main actors visible are Hugh Grant, Leonardo di Caprio, Kate Winslet and Mel Gibson.

Go through the different kinds of movies, checking that students understand the descriptions. *A weepie* is a film that makes you cry a lot, and if students are unsure of *a sci-fi thing*, you could refer them to the photo from *Robocop* on page 113. *A cult movie* is a film that is very popular among a certain group of people. For example, *The Blair Witch Project* quickly became a cult. Have students work in pairs for the matching task. You might want to teach the expression *It's a cross between a (comedy) and (a sci-fi thing)* as some films obviously do not fit into simple categories.

When students have finished, write the seven categories in a row on the board and ask the class to suggest other examples for each one.

2   Asking questions about films

These are typical questions that are asked about films or television programmes and should be learned as whole expressions. Remind students that they may want to add some of these expressions to their notebooks. At this stage, just get students to complete the exercise, as pronunciation and practice is dealt with in the exercises that follow.

After students have read the examples in the **Real English** note on *some*, see if they can come up with an example sentence of their own. You could also point out that *some* used in this way often suggests that you don't think it's worth mentioning the name of the person. For example:

A: *Who was that on the phone?*
B: *Some guy from work. He's locked himself in again and wants the keys.*

A: *What's this programme?*
B: *Some old professor talking about world conflicts. It's not worth watching.*

3   And when you can't answer!

This exercise focuses on useful expressions for when you can't remember the name of something or someone. Have students work individually, reminding them that the first word of the expression is capitalised. Then play the recording for students to follow as a model. Have them practise the expressions several times until they can say them naturally. Finally, check that students understand the meaning by answering questions a–c.

4   Pronunciation

Have students practise the conversations in **2 Asking questions about films** in pairs. Then play the recording so that they can hear the expressions. You might want to talk about how these expressions are said almost like one word, with each word being linked to the next. This kind of linking is most noticeable when a word ends in a consonant and the one next to it ends in a vowel. For example:

Who's in it?
Where's it on?
What's it about?

Have students practise these questions, trying to link the words smoothly. Next, get the students in pairs to talk about some films they've seen. Remind them that they can respond with any of the expressions from **3 And when you can't answer!** when they can't remember the details.

5   Film vocabulary

You could lead into this task by writing the word *film* on the board and eliciting or providing a few interesting adjectives (e.g. *epic, low-budget, black-and-white*) and noun collocations (*film + buff, crew, critic, festival*). For the exercise, students can work in pairs, using their dictionaries when necessary. Ask questions as you check their answers, to generate connected language. For example:
Can you tell me some other famous directors?
What else do governments ban? (books, demonstrations)
Why else might they cut part of a film?

Remind students to add the expressions they find useful to their notebooks.

Answers

1. director 2. banned 3. stars 4. special effects 5. cut
6. dubbed 7. dialogue 8. soundtrack 9. plot
10. ending 11. set 12. scene

You might need to explain a couple of the expressions:

- If a *dialogue is sharp and witty*, it is both clever and funny.
- If a *plot has lots of twists and turns*, the story has lots of unexpected events.

6 Speaking

These questions provide a personalised follow-up to **5 Film vocabulary** and consolidate the meaning of the new vocabulary. Do the exercise in pairs or small groups. Here are some further questions you might get students to answer:

Do you know of any films that have been banned in your country? Why? Do you agree with the decision?

Do you ever go and see a film just because it stars your favourite actor/actress or because it is by your favourite director?

Who's your favourite director or actor/actress? Why?

How important is the plot of a film to you? Can you think of a film that had a great plot in the beginning but was a let-down by the ending?

Reading

1 Before you read

Lead in to the reading text by discussing these questions as a class. Then refer students to the photo from *Robocop* on page 113. Ask if anyone recognises this science fiction film about a prototype law-enforcing robot that goes out of control and causes havoc. (*Robo* from *robot* and *cop* from *copper* – slang for police officer.) Ask if anyone has seen the film and if they liked it and whether they thought it was very violent.

2 While you read (TV Robocop not violent enough for viewers)

Explain that the article the students are going to read is about when *Robocop* was shown on British TV. Ask them to read the article to find out the answers to the three questions. When they've finished reading, they can discuss their answers in pairs.

Answers

1. Because too much violence had been cut.
2. It ruined the film. It was difficult to follow the plot.
3. Mary Whitehouse set up the National Viewers' and Listeners' Association (NVLA) in the late sixties to protest against sex and violence on TV. The NVLA feels that cutting the violence from a film like *Robocop* is good for society as a whole, and that the people who complained are just thinking about themselves.

Real English

Bad language or swear words are often avoided in English courses, but are common in real-life conversation. However, with the increasing incidence of swear words in films, newspapers and even on BBC television, which is renowned for high standards and quality programming, it is important that students are familiar with swear words and their common substitutes, such as *fuck* (when written) or *the f-word* when spoken. It is also useful to know how to report how somebody swore at you: *He told me to f-off.* You might like to ask if strong swear words are common in films, television and papers in the students' own culture(s) and how people feel about this. Remind students that using language like this can cause offence, and if they use it with people they don't know, they do risk offending them.

3 Collocations

Students should try to complete the summary without referring back to the text. They can then reread the article to confirm their answers. Remind them to add these collocations to their notebooks.

Answers

1. strong public reaction
2. local television station
3. follow the plot
4. classic example
5. climate
6. violence

4 Speaking

Give students time to do this exercise on their own before they discuss it in pairs. Alternatively, after students do it on their own, let them mingle, trying to find the student with the views closest to their own. You might want to teach some expressions which show strong disagreement (as long as students realise that these expressions are strong!):

That's ridiculous!

That's rubbish.

What a load of rubbish!

That's just not true.

Oh, come on!

And of course, some expressions for agreeing:

That's true, actually.

I agree with that …

I couldn't agree more. I couldn't have said it better.

Students could choose one of the statements 1–6 to write about for homework.

Using grammar

1 Past perfect simple

This exercise focuses on how the past perfect is often used when we want to connect an action in the past with another earlier action, the earlier action being in the past perfect. If it helps your students, you can represent this relationship with a timeline on the board. Students can work on this exercise individually while you walk around checking answers. Point out that the contracted form *I'd* is common in spoken English. Select a few students to read their sentences to the class. Write these two patterns on the board:

I'd never … before.

I'd … once before.

Encourage students to copy them in their notebooks along with a few examples from this page. Tell them to review the explanation of the past perfect in the **Grammar commentary, G26 Pest perfect simple** on page 165 when they have finished.

Answers
Probable answers:
2. I'd never made a speech
3. I'd never met them
4. I'd never had/tried it
5. He'd been married
6. They'd died in
7. We'd just had
8. I'd never actually flown

2 Practice

In the personalisation task, some of the sentences will obviously not apply to the students, but ask them to invent a way to complete them or tell them to ignore them and think of two or three different ones themselves. Put students in pairs to have brief conversations about their statements. Select a student to give an example first:

Student: *I'd never had prawns until I went to a Chinese restaurant.*

Teacher: *And did you like them?*

Student: *No, not really.*

Teacher: *Why not?*

Student: *Well, I've never really liked seafood and this was no exception.*

Using vocabulary

1 I've heard it's really good

These conversations are about films that the speakers haven't seen, but are thinking about going to see. Point out to students that a lot of the highlighted language could also be used to talk about other things that people are thinking of seeing, reading or even buying. Once students have finished the reordering task, read the conversations out loud so they can hear how the expressions sound, particularly the intonation patterns. Students can then practise reading the conversations in pairs.

Answers
Conversation 1: 1. b.   2. a.   3. c   4. d.
Conversation 2: 1. a.   2. c.   3. b.   4. d.
Conversation 3: 1. d.   2. b.   3. a.   4. e.   5. c.

2 Speaking

do warmer again activity using vocab

One approach to this freer practice is to put students in threes, with the third person listening for the highlighted expressions and awarding a point for each expression they hear. The winner then becomes the listener/scorer and so on.

3 | Television vocabulary

This exercise focuses on several words and collocations connected with television. Students could do this exercise on their own, using a dictionary when necessary and then comparing their answers in pairs. You may need to explain that the *BBC* stands for the *British Broadcasting Corporation* and *ITV* stands for *Independent Television*. Have students underline expressions and collocations in the text and add them to their notebooks.

Answers

1. remote 2. channel 3. advertisements 4. aerials
5. digital/cable 6. cable/digital 7. documentaries
8. series

4 | Speaking

Students could answer these questions either in small groups or as a whole class. Point out *switch the television off* and give some other examples of things we can *switch on* and *off* (lights, vacuum cleaner, the news).

5 | Audiences

Students may want an explicit definition for these terms:
- *Spectators* are the people watching a live sporting event.
- *Fans* are people who follow a certain band or support a sports team.
- *A congregation* is in a church.
- *An audience* is usually at a live performance (opera, plays, live TV shows).
- *On-lookers* are people who see something happening, like an accident.
- *Viewers* are people watching TV.

Note: Hakkinen is a Finnish Formula 1 race driver.

Answers

1. audience 2. congregation 3. fans 4. viewers
5. spectators 6. on-lookers

Using grammar

1 | Mixed conditionals

Students will probably be familiar with the three traditional conditional structures. Here, however, they are introduced to an example of a 'mixed conditional'. Remind students of the article on *Robocop* and then let them think about the difference between *would be* and *would have been*. Make sure they see that *would have* expresses an imaginary or hypothetical past result, whereas *would* expresses an imaginary or hypothetical present result.

Have the students work on the sentences 1–6 individually before checking their answers. You may need to explain that *in a (terrible) state* describes the poor condition of something (e.g. the country, the roads) or someone (e.g. you, my father). Ask students to come up with things that might prompt someone to say *The country is in a terrible state*.

Answers

Present imaginary result: 2, 3, 5, 6
Past imaginary result: 1, 4

Students can now think of who the people being discussed in 1–6 might be. They don't have to come up with actual names, just something like these:
He's probably someone who convinced him to stay on at school.
She must be some kind of politician.

While checking the answers to the sentences 7–12, make sure students use the contracted form *'d* where appropriate. You might need to explain a few expressions:
- The money you receive from the state or a private company when you retire from work is called *a pension*. For example: *At what age do you start getting a pension in your country?*
- Federico Fellini was an Italian film director. His films include *La Strada* and *La Dolce Vita*.
- *The Dark Ages* is a reference to the time in European history after the collapse of the Roman Empire. If you say someone or a group of people are *still living in the Dark Ages*, it means you think they live or think in an uncivilised or uncultured way.

Answers

7. I'd never have gone
8. I wouldn't have had
9. you wouldn't be getting
10. I'd never have got into
11. we'd still be living in the Dark Ages
12. nothing would have gone wrong, we'd still be married

After students have finished writing five sentences about people who influenced their life or their country, and talked about them to a partner, choose a few examples to put on the board. You might want to give some personal examples first.

2 Speaking

This speaking task provides another opportunity to use the mixed conditional structure. Make sure students know who these people are and what they are famous for. Write a few patterns on the board to help:

If it hadn't been for … , (we) wouldn't …

If it hadn't been for … , (we)'d still…

… had a enormous/considerable/influence on the world/society.

Answers

Possible sentences:

If it hadn't been for Thomas Edison, the electric light bulb and the gramophone wouldn't have been invented.

If it hadn't been for Elvis, rock'n'roll would never have become so popular.

If it hadn't been for Mikhail Gorbachev, the Soviet Union would still exist.

If it hadn't been for Albert Einstein, we wouldn't have nuclear weapons.

If it hadn't been for Marie Curie, millions more people would die of disease every year.

If it hadn't been for George Bush, the United Nations would still be influential.

If it hadn't been for Gandhi, India wouldn't have gained its independence when it did.

If it hadn't been for Mother Teresa, life would be much worse for thousands of people in Calcutta.

Review: Units 13–16

The exercises here can be used as a quiz. **4 Speaking** and **6 Look back and check: Recommending**, however, are better done as a discussion in pairs.

1 Tenses

Answers

1. I went   2. I've played   3. Have you been staying in
4. I've asked   5. must've been   6. I've been trying
7. Did you speak   8. must be   9. I haven't seen
10. I hadn't done

2 Multiple choice

Answers

1. b.   2. a.   3. b.   4. a.   5. b.   6. b.   7. b.   8. b.

3 Mixed conditionals, *I wish I'd ...*

Answers

1. c.   2. a.   3. f.   4. b.   5. d.   6. e.

4 Speaking

Answers will vary.

5 Conversation

Answers

1. a.   2. d.   3. f.   4. e.   5. c.   6. b.

6 Look back and check: Recommending

Answers will vary.

7 Expressions

Answers

1. It's not worth the entrance fee
2. get a life
3. he's not exactly
4. a sore point
5. that reminds me
6. I haven't seen you for ages

8 Collocations

Answers

1. e.   2. h.   3. b.   4. g.   5. f.   6. c.   7. a.   8. d.
9. m.   10. i.   11. n.   12. k.   13. o.   14. p.   15. j.
16. l.

9 Real English

Answers

1. e.   2. a.   3. d.   4. b.   5. g.   6. c.   7. f.

10 Idioms

Answers

1. d.   2. h.   3. g.   4. a.   5. b.   6. f.   7. e.   8. c.

11 What can you remember?

Answers will vary.

12 Vocabulary quiz

Answers

1. No. It means you can't see the purpose of it.
2. They look for motives.
3. It makes you cry.
4. Answers will vary. Possibilities are: muscles, something made of stone, old bread.
5. Yes.
6. In the future/in space.
7. Answers will vary. Possibilities are: a relationship, an argument, an illness.
8. Answers will vary. Possibilities are: cucumbers, onions.
9. No. They decide if the film is suitable for different age groups, etc., and maybe cut parts or even ban the whole film.
10. No.
11. A still life is a painting of objects. A portrait is a painting of a person.
12. It means over-the-top.
13. In the past, usually 100 years ago or more.
14. No. You've known them for a long time.
15. Answers will vary. Possibilities are: riot, accident, a lot of damage/suffering/harm/problems.
16. The word *plot* is used specifically when talking about the events in a book, a play or a film, so it is a more specific use than the more general word *story*.
17. You find them in your life.
18. No. You are saying you think it's OK for them to do something.
19. Yes.
20. It was made in Hollywood.

Learner advice: The authors speak!

Answers will vary.

Unit overview

General topic
Problems and changes in cities.

Dialogue
Chris and Claire give their views on a local traffic problem.

Language input
- Driving vocabulary: *take a wrong turn, slam on the brakes*, etc.
- Making suggestions: *It'd be more useful if they built a multi-storey*, etc.
- Expressions for giving opinions and disagreeing: *I think it's a great idea, Yes, but don't forget that … ,* etc.
- City vocabulary: *cosmopolitan, inner city*, etc.
- The passive: *The streets are never cleaned round here.*
- Impersonal *they*: *They should do something about it.*
- Animal idioms: *I do all the donkey work*, etc.

Language strip

Have students choose any expressions they find interesting and, on their own, find out more about them. In a later class, ask them to share the information. For a small group activity, ask them to choose three expressions and come up with a situation that might prompt someone to say them. Alternatively, ask them to find expressions containing *it* (e.g. *It's a major issue*) or *that* (e.g. *That would be far better*) and suggest what those words refer to. You might need to explain some of the following expressions:

- *Sleeping policemen* in British English refers to the *speed bumps* in the road that help to slow traffic down.
- If you describe a place as *crazy*, you're saying it's crowded. For example: *I wouldn't go into the city centre today. It's crazy there on the weekend.*
- If you add *full stop* to an opinion, you are strengthening it by implying there is no discussion about it.

Remind students to record any of the expressions that they like in their notebooks.

Lead in

Use the photographs on page 120 to lead in to the topic of traffic problems. Ask if students know what the people in the top picture do. (They are traffic wardens, who in the UK put parking tickets on illegally parked cars.) Ask who does the equivalent job in the students' countries, and what exactly they do. Here are some further questions:
Has anyone had a parking ticket? How much did you have to pay?
Do you think speed humps are useful? Do they really work?

Listening

1 | Traffic survey

Before looking at the list, ask the students what sort of traffic problems they have in their own towns or cities. Then put them into small groups and ask them to list as many solutions to traffic problems as they can think of. Then get them to compare their lists with the list in the Coursebook. Check that students understand the words and expressions. You may need to explain that *accident black spots* are places where a lot of accidents tend to occur. Point out the **Real English** note on *sleeping policemen*. There are a lot of useful collocations in the list to point out to students: *install speed cameras, accident black spots, quiet streets, on-street parking* (as opposed to parking in car parks)*, pedestrianise the main shopping area, provide better public transport, ban all cars from the town centre, double the number of, a one-way system.*

Before pairs of students discuss the list, write some sentence starters on the board to help:
The best way to deal with traffic problems would be to …
That wouldn't really work because …
That would be a waste of time because …
I think it might/would be better to …

Collect the four solutions with the highest priority from each group and write them on the board. Then as a class, work out which approach to improving traffic problems is the most popular.

2 | While you listen (More sleeping policemen!)

Introduce the listening task by setting the scene. Have students read the two questions and then play the recording, making sure they cover the text. They can then discuss their answers in pairs.

> **Answers**
>
> 1. The speed of cars; a pedestrian crossing in the wrong place; too many cars parked near the crossing.
> 2. Move the crossing and put sleeping policemen or speed cameras on the road to slow the traffic down.

With a partner, students see if they can fill in the first two or three gaps in the conversation from memory. Play the recording again for them to fill in the rest of the missing words. Pause the recording so they have time to write in what they hear. Finally, play the recording again with students listening while reading the tapescript on page 155. The missing words are highlighted. Refer students to the two **Real English** notes on *I mean* and *penalty points*. Encourage students to underline any expressions in the conversation that they find interesting and to record them in their notebooks.

3 | Driving vocabulary

One way of exploiting this text is to ask students to close their Coursebooks, and write the missing words in the list on the board. Then read the text stopping at each blank. Students then write down the phrase including the word from the list. for example, *I'd taken a wrong turning,* on a piece of paper. They can then compare their answers with a partner. Finally, they can follow in their Coursebooks as you read the text a second time with the answers. Remind students to transfer these expressions to their notebooks.

> **Answers**
>
> 1. turning 2. direction 3. U-turn 4. one-way street
> 5. headlights 6. brakes 7. pull over 8. petrol
>
> The collocations are:
>
> 1. take a wrong turning
> 2. go in the wrong direction
> 3. do a U-turn
> 4. go down a one-way street
> 5. slam on the brakes
> 6. run out of petrol

4 | Speaking

This exercise gives students practice in using some of the vocabulary from **3 Driving vocabulary**. Talk about any personal experiences first, encouraging the class to ask you questions. Students can then talk about the questions in small groups. You might want to give them of a list of ways to describe driving conditions. For example:

heavy/light traffic
It's murder finding somewhere to park.
You're taking your life into your own hands.

Using grammar

1 | Second conditionals for making suggestions

The second conditional structure is often used to make suggestions. The suggestion of what to do follows *if*. Have students read the example and then get them to match 1–4 to a–d to make short dialogues. While checking their answers explain that if we describe traffic as *absolute chaos*, we're saying that the driving conditions are very bad because of so many cars, and that *a multi-storey* is short for *a multi-storey car park*.

> **Answers**
>
> 1. d.   2. b.   3. a.   4. c.

For the second group of sentences, you might need to explain that in many places in Britain there are closed circuit televisions. Ask if this is the case in students' countries.

> **Answers**
>
> 5. g.   6. h.   7. f.   8. e.

2 | Sentence starters

Have students underline the sentence starters in the eight short dialogues in **1 Second conditionals for making suggestions** – each expression occurs twice – and then write them out in the space provided. Each of these expressions needs to be learned as a single item of vocabulary, so say each one, paying particular attention to the contractions. Have students repeat them chorally and individually until they can say them fluently. One way to practise them is to write them on the board and gradually erase more and more words, seeing if students can still remember the expressions.

Answers

1. It'd be more useful if …
2. What would be really great is if …
3. I think it'd be a really good idea if …
4. It'd be (far) better if …

3 Practice

Students can now read the eight short dialogues in **1 Second conditionals for making suggestions** in pairs. When they have finished, get them to work with another partner making other suggestions about the problems. Give an example first so that they can see how to do this. For example:

A: *This town's dead at night, isn't it?*

B: *It's not exactly Times Square! It'd be far better if there were a few more cafés and bars.*

Finally, refer students to the **Grammar commentary, G28 Second conditionals for making suggestions** on page 166.

Using vocabulary

1 Collocations

Lead in to this exercise by referring back to the expression *It'd be a really good idea.* Ask students for other adjectives that could be used to describe *idea* (e.g. *bad, brilliant, great*). You can then explain that this exercise will give them more practice with collocations, as well as providing some more expressions for talking about their views on things. If you have time, you might see if the students can use their dictionaries to find two more verb and/or adjective collocations for each noun. Good monolingual dictionaries usually contain such collocations in the example sentences for the headword.

Answers

1. (a) difficult (question) 2. strong (views) 3. tackle (that problem) 4. raises (the question of) 5. cause (problems) 6. (a) major (issue) 7. different (views) 8. avoid (the issue)

Students should record the individual collocations (e.g. *a difficult question, strong views*) as well as the whole sentences because these are complete expressions that they can learn and use in other situations. Have small groups discuss the questions at the end of the exercise for further practice with these collocations.

2 Personal opinions

This exercise gives several ways to introduce a personal opinion. Say the expressions for the students and ask them to mark which words receive the main stress. They can then practise saying them themselves. Show how these expressions would work in a few examples:

A: *What do you think about this idea of pubs being allowed to open for twenty-four hours?*

B: *Personally, I think it's brilliant!*

A: *Have you heard they're going to ban smoking on buses?*

B: *As far as I'm concerned, they can ban smoking everywhere!*

For the pair work activity, you might need to point out the *kilt*, as worn by Scottish men, in the photo. To help in the discussion, teach the expression *It's a good idea in theory, but in practice …* and give an example:

One car per family is a good idea in theory, but in practice it'll never work because public transport isn't reliable enough.

3 Role play

Before you do this exercise, give students time to look through the language in the previous exercises, and perhaps also look through their own notebooks. You could also create a gap-fill exercise by writing the expressions you want the students to revise on the board, but leaving out the occasional word and then asking students to complete the whole expression. For example:

What … be really … is if …

That's a … question to …

Use gap words which are fairly easy to remember; this is an activity to jog the memory, not to test students.

Before you begin the role play, explain the following:

• *A colleague* is someone you work with.

• If a bank is *old-fashioned*, its working conditions and ideas are what used to be normal in the past but are no longer so.

• A *network system* refers to how computers in many businesses are typically linked together to allow sharing of files and resources.

Then divide the class into groups of three if possible. Set the scene by telling them that they are having a drink after work and are discussing the things that they are not happy about. Write the opening sentence on the board for the first person to start with:

You know, I just can't believe that we're still using those computers …

The others join in and they all make suggestions on improving the situation before one of them raises the next problem on the list and so on.

Encourage students to use the expressions during the activity by walking around the class and feeding in appropriate expressions where students are having difficulty. Give feedback on how the groups performed and then ask them to do the role play again, putting your feedback into practice.

The final question could be discussed as a whole class activity. Give students two minutes to think about the question and then let individuals who have something to say tell the class.

4 Disagreeing

This exercise introduces some expressions used for disagreeing. Have individuals put the words in the right order, reminding them that the first word in each expression is capitalised. Then play the recording so that students can check their answers and hear the pronunciation. Have them practise saying the expressions.

Before getting pairs to disagree with the statements, give an example of how the conversation might go:

A: *There's too much sport on TV, isn't there?*
B: *Yes, but don't forget a lot of people actually like watching it.*
A: *But do you really think so many people like watching golf?*

For the second stage, practise the intonation of *Oh, yes, I know what you mean* (agreeing) in contrast to *Yes, I know what you mean, but …* (disagreeing). Again, you could give an example first:

A: *There's too much sport on TV, isn't there?*
B: *Oh yes, I know what you mean. I can't believe how much golf there is.*

Answers
1. Well, I agree up to a point, but …
2. Yes, I know what you mean, but …
3. Yes, but don't you think that …
4. Yes, but don't forget that …

5 Talking about cities

This exercise gives students some ways of describing different kinds and parts of cities. Lead in by describing a couple of cities that you know. Try to use some of the vocabulary in the box so that students have some exposure to the words before they do the exercise. You might want to explain that *every nationality under the sun* is an idiomatic expression emphasising that there is a wide variety of nationalities, *bedsits* are flats with just one room, and *medieval* refers to the historical period of the Middle Ages from about the eleventh century to the mid fifteenth century. Refer students to the **Real English** note for *inner city* and the alternative *city centre*.

Answers
1. capital 2. industrial 3. cosmopolitan 4. inner city
5. historic 6. shanty towns 7. centre 8. overcrowded

6 Speaking

Have students discuss these questions in small groups. You could write some patterns on the board to help:

… is the most historic/cosmopolitan city I've been to in my life.

… is heavily industrialised/severely overcrowded.

Using grammar

1 The passive

Ask if the students have ever heard of the famous English town of Brighton and if they can tell you anything about it. Give them some more information: *Brighton is a popular seaside town on the south coast, about fifty miles south of London. It has a lot of visitors, so it has a lot of restaurants, bars and clubs. The club scene is one of the liveliest outside London. Many people have heard of Brighton because of Graham Green's novel, 'Brighton Rock'. Lots of buildings have recently been modernised or have changed their use. In particular, several banks have now become restaurants or bars.*

Ask if the students' own cities have undergone any major changes recently such as more cafés, more pedestrian areas or more trendy bars. Explain that *trendy* means fashionable/popular. You can wear *trendy clothes*, it can be *trendy to do something*, you can also describe people as *trendy*. Go over the two example sentences and practise the pronunciation of the patterns:
It used to be a …
It's been turned into a …

Do the first passive sentence together in class, then put students in pairs for numbers 2–4.

Answers
1. It used to be an estate agent's. It's been turned into a restaurant.
2. It used to be an insurance office. It's been turned into a trendy bar.
3. It used to be a bank. It's been turned into a fish and chip restaurant.
4. It used to be a public toilet. It's been turned into a sandwich bar.

For the personalisation questions at the end of the exercise, go over the additional patterns and practise them. Give some examples of a place that you know first before having students work in small groups. Encourage students to give their opinions of the changes.

2 | Grammar check

Take one of the examples from **1 The passive**, *It's been turned into a video shop,* to illustrate how and why passives are used. First ask the class if they know who turned the bank into a video shop, (e.g. some builders? the owner?) and whether the speaker wants to focus on those people or on the fact that the bank is now a video shop. Explain that because the speaker wants to focus on the latter, a passive is used in preference to an active.

We also use a passive when the doer of the action is unknown. For example:
My wallet's been stolen.

We can use a passive when the doer is understood by the listener:
We've been given a pay rise.

In the sentences in this exercise, the doer of the action is a group of nameless people, and so can either be expressed with *they* or by a passive. The choice of a passive would show that the speaker wants to focus more on the result than on the people doing the action. When students have finished the exercise, have them read the **Grammar commentary, G29 The passive** on page 166.

Answers

1. An old bomb's been found in the town centre.
2. The High Street's been closed.
3. The swimming pool's being cleaned today.
4. A multi-storey car park's being built.
5. The rubbish is collected on Wednesdays.
6. The streets are never cleaned round here.
7. That restaurant was closed down last year.
8. Rats were found in the kitchen.
9. The toilets were still being cleaned when the Queen arrived.
10. The road was being repaired all last week.
11. A new airport's going to be built.
12. The street lighting's going to be improved.
13. Something should be done about all the litter.
14. A zebra crossing should be put there.

---

3 | Idioms focus

The focus here is on the use of the names of animals in several idiomatic expressions. Unlike *zebra crossing,* the reason for the choice of animal is sometimes rather obscure. When students have finished completing the sentences 1–8, have them record the idioms that they like in their notebooks, along with an appropriate translation.

Answers

1. dogs 2. horse 3. donkey 4. fish 5. cat 6. cows
7. sheep 8. goose

You may need to explain a little more about some of these idioms:

- If a place *is going to the dogs*, it is becoming less popular and isn't as good as it was in the past. You can also talk about *the country going to the dogs*.

- If you describe someone as *a bit of a dark horse*, you are surprised by something they have done or can do because previously you didn't know much about them.

- If you *do all the donkey work*, you do the more difficult part of a job that requires physical labour.

- If you *feel like a fish out of water*, you feel uncomfortable because you are in an unfamiliar situation.

- If you *let the cat out of the bag* you reveal a secret.

- If you say someone *could do something until the cows come home*, they could do it for a very long time if they had the chance.

- If you are considered *the black sheep of the family*, you do things differently from other people in the family. It often implies that what you do is considered bad.

- If you say that you were sent *on a wild goose chase*, you are complaining that you wasted a lot of time looking for something because you were given misleading information about where it was. Possibly, it doesn't even exist!

Photo opportunity

The cartoon of the black sheep of the family could be used to remind students about making note cards with a picture on one side and the idiomatic expression, translation and an example of it used in context on the other. The note cards could be used for review in a later class.

18 | Annoying things

Unit overview

General topic
Things that annoy you.

Reading
Two examples of how to tackle the problems caused by chewing gum.

Language input
- Phrasal verbs: *not going to put up with it any more, get way with murder,* etc.
- Complaining with *was/were going to: I thought it was going to be a five-star hotel, but … .*
- Expressions for complaining: *I wish they wouldn't, That's the last thing I need,* etc.
- Some fixed expressions for responding to complaints: *It's not the end of the world, Don't let it get you down,* etc.
- Expressions with *bother: You needn't bother, I can't be bothered,* etc.
- Idioms for describing problem situations: *It's a Catch 22 situation, It's a vicious circle,* etc.

Language strip

Have students choose any expressions they find interesting and, on their own, find out more about them. In a later class, ask them to share the information. For a small group activity, ask them to find expressions you can say to someone who is annoyed (e.g. *Calm down*). You can also ask them to find expressions with *it* (e.g. *It really bugs me*) or *that* (e.g. *I wish he wouldn't do that*) and suggest what *it* and *that* refer to. You might need to explain some of the following expressions:

- If something *really bugs you*, it really annoys you. For example: *It really bugs me when people put their feet up on the seats in buses.*
- If you *go on about something*, you keep on complaining about something. For example: *I wish people wouldn't keep going on about the weather all the time.*
- You would say *That's the last thing I need* to complain when you hear about something that has happened or that you need to do when you have other things to worry about as well. For example: *The last thing I need at the moment is another thing going wrong with the house.*

- If something *makes your blood boil*, it makes you very annoyed. For example: *It really makes my blood boil to think of all the money they spend on weapons.*

Remind students to record any of the expressions that they like in their notebooks.

Lead in

One way to lead in to the topic of annoying things is to ask each student to write on a piece of paper one thing that really annoys them. Write one yourself too. Collect all the slips of paper, mix them all up, and deal out one slip per student. Everyone should then go around asking the question *So, are you the one who's really annoyed by … ?* until they find the person who wrote their slip. Once the person has been found, students can sit down. You can then explain that in this unit, they will learn how to talk and complain about things that annoy them.

Reading

1 | Before you read

Start by asking the class to look up the word *sticky* in their dictionaries. Draw attention to how in the expressions *sticky situation* and *sticky problem, sticky* means *difficult.* Then, ask students to look at the photograph and ask if the scene of all the chewing gum stains looks familiar. See if they can therefore explain the pun in the title of the reading text. You can then discuss the questions as a class. You may need to explain that *tackle a problem* means *try to deal with a problem.* You can also *tackle an issue.* Encourage students to make suggestions with some of the second conditional structures from the previous unit. For example: *It'd be a really good idea if they just banned it altogether.*

2 | While you read (A sticky problem)

Explain to students that they are going to read an article on how two places have tackled this problem and they are to decide which way they like best. Have them discuss their ideas in pairs. Encourage them to use some of the expressions from the previous unit for expressing their views. For example: *I think it's brilliant/ridiculous.*

3 Comprehension check

Get students in pairs to try to recall the expressions from the text to correct the sentences. Tell them not to worry about those they can't remember. When they've done as much as they can, let them reread the text to confirm or correct their answers. As you go through the answers, ask a few questions to generate more connected language. For example:

Do you know any famous people who have had face lifts?

What other nouns could we use after 'flooded with'? (cheap imports, enquiries)

What has this country banned the importing of?

What are some other words we can use before 'penalty'? (the death penalty, the maximum penalty)

What is another policy that has been a great success?

What political things can be lifted? (sanctions, restrictions)

Remind students to add these collocations, and any other expressions they find useful from the article, to their notebooks.

> **Answers**
>
> 1. The town recently underwent a £1 million face-lift.
> 2. The council have been flooded with complaints.
> 3. Singapore banned the importing of chewing gum.
> 4. There are severe penalties for breaking the anti-chewing gum law.
> 5. The policy has been a great success.
> 6. The ban will be partially lifted.

4 Speaking

Get the students into small groups to discuss these questions. Again, you might want to write some of the expressions for giving opinions, agreeing and disagreeing from the previous unit on the board.

Using vocabulary

1 Phrasal verbs

Start off by asking the class what *isn't going to put up with any more* means in the example (they are going to start doing something about it). Then get students to complete the matching exercise. While going through the answers, check that they understand the meaning of the phrasal verbs by paraphrasing the sentence. For example:

get away with such awful service = provide a bad service, but have no negative consequences as a result of it

goes on about her silly little problems = keeps complaining about her problems, which aren't very serious

> **Answers**
>
> 1. d.   2. e.   3. c.   4. b.   5. a.

Read the sentences, asking the students to listen for which part of the phrasal verb you are stressing before having the class practise reading the sentences to each other in pairs. You may need to explain that *just look at the state of it* means *look at what a bad condition it is in*. You can also say *Look at the state we're/you're in*.

The next task provides students with two extra contexts for each of these phrasal verbs. Have students work individually before comparing their answers in pairs.

> **Answers**
>
> 6a. end up 6b. end up 7a. put up with 7b. put up with
> 8a. get away with 8b. get away with 9a. mess up
> 9b. mess up 10a. going on about 10b. going on about

Tell students to go back and underline the expressions, noticing the patterns verbs occur in. Write the patterns on the board:

end up + -ing form
put up with + noun + -ing form
get away with + noun
mess up + noun
going on about how + clause

Encourage students to record these patterns along with some of the examples from the exercise. For example:

If (something doesn't change/improve), I'm going to end up going mad.

How can you put up with him treating you like that?

if I thought I could get away with it

get away with murder (ask how many of the 'death-related' expressions they remember from Unit 11)

Use the questions at the end of the exercise to reinforce some of the expressions.

2 Speaking

This exercise uses the phrasal verb *put up with* to introduce the topic of complaining, which is the focus of the next few exercises. First ask students, either as a class, or in groups of two or three, to say whether they would complain in these situations or not. Write the following expressions on the board and encourage students to use them during the discussion:

I probably wouldn't say anything.
I'd complain immediately.
I'd just put up with it, I think.
I'm not sure what I would do.
It depends on the situation.

Next, ask students in pairs to choose four of the situations and write what they would say if they did complain. Help students, supplying the expressions they need to complain appropriately, and conduct a general class feedback on which expressions to use in these situations. These mini-dialogues could form the basis for short role plays at the end of the lesson, or at the start of the next one, to recycle language from the unit.

Using grammar

1 Was/were going to

It is often useful for students to see how grammatical structures work within a functional context, so here the focus is on how the structure *was/were going to* can be used to complain about things that were contrary to our expectations. Lead in by asking the class whether they have ever been on a holiday where things didn't turn out the way they had expected. After listening to any stories, explain that they are going to read about a holiday from hell. Have students suggest what things could go wrong on an organised holiday. Then have them read the three examples. Ask them to tell you the patterns that they notice and write them on the board:
I thought … was/were going to … but …
… said … was/were going to … but …

Then have students complete the sentences 1–9, reminding them that 7–9 require a passive. After going through their answers, encourage students to record these patterns and a few of the examples from this exercise, or the personalised ones in the next, in their notebooks.

Answers

1. were going to stay
2. was going to be
3. was going to be
4. was going to be
5. was going to have
6. were going to have
7. were going to be met
8. were going to be changed
9. were going to be taken

2 Your complaints

This exercise personalises and consolidates the structure introduced in **1 Was/were going to**. Have students work alone completing the sentences 1–5 before having them get together with a partner to share and explain their answers. Have a few students read out their sentences before talking about any of your own personal experiences. Refer students to the **Real English** note on *haircut/hairdo* and *having your hair done*. Ask them what else is involved in having your hair done (e.g. *having a perm, having highlights*). This might be a good time to review the hairstyle vocabulary from Unit 11. Ask students to describe the hairdos in the photographs on page 129.

Answers

Possible answers:

1. I thought it was going to be a little bit curly, but this is ridiculous.
2. I thought I was going to lose weight quickly, but I ended up gaining weight instead.
3. I thought it was going to be reliable, but I've had so many problems with it.
4. I thought it was going to be a comedy, but it was more like a thriller.
5. I thought it was going to be on at ten o'clock, but they'd changed it to eleven.

You can follow up by asking students for any other real-life experiences they can share, reminding them to add time expressions where necessary. For example:
Last Monday I thought I was going to be late for my English class, but I wasn't.

When I was younger, I always thought I was going to be rich and famous, but now I'm just a teacher.

Remind students to review this structure in the **Grammar commentary, G30 Was/were going to** on page 166.

Using vocabulary

1 Complaining about things

Either have students fill in the gaps in both conversations straight away, or have them listen to each conversation twice with their Coursebooks closed before filling in the answers.

Answers

1. Complaining about a meal

1. It would've been OK if that was the only problem, but

2. And then, to top the whole thing off,

3. they made it sound as if

2. Complaining about a situation

1. I've got a bit of a problem with

2. I mean, the last thing I need

3. I wish they wouldn't

Practise saying the individual phrases before getting students into pairs to practise the conversations. Remind them to sound annoyed! Give another example of *the last thing I need* to help students understand how this expression is used:

I've been working hard all day and I'm exhausted. The last thing I need is to come home and find that all our relations are here.

A similar expression to *And to top the whole thing off, …* is *And to make matters worse, … .*

2 | Practice

Allow students time to think of what they want to say and to review the language they need to say it. You might want them to write their complaints to begin with and to do the task two or three times, each time relying less on their notes. Provide the following example to give students an idea of what you want:

I went round to Liz's place last night. She made it sound as if it was really close to the town centre, but I got totally lost. First of all, I took the wrong turning off the motorway, then I went up a one-way street the wrong way. The map was useless.

In the second part of this exercise, students role-play a situation from their own experience. Refer them to the **Real English** note on *get it off your chest*. Ask whether they tend to *get things off their chest* or to *keep things bottled up*. A fun way to extend this activity is to have a complaining knock-out competition. Ask for two volunteers. They each have a turn to complain in front of the class using one of the situations. The class decides who the best complainer is. The winner then has another turn to complain about another situation, competing against the next volunteer and so on. This continues until all volunteers have had a turn complaining and have been knocked out except the one remaining student, who is the best complainer.

3 | It really drives me mad

This exercise takes this language area a step further and introduces a number of expressions that are typical responses when people are complaining to us. See if students can work out the meaning of the idiom *It really drives me mad*. Can they think of any other similar expressions? (*It drives me up the wall.*)

Complete the first dialogue together as an example. Ask students for another word for *bug* (annoy), and *bother* (worry) before referring them to the **Real English** note on page 131. Then play the recording and let students check their answers. Next, they can practise the short dialogues in pairs. Encourage them to keep the conversation going. Ask students which two expressions sound more sympathetic (*Don't worry* and *It's not the end of the world, Don't let it get you down*). You may need to explain that if you are *short-listed for a job*, you have been chosen to be in the final group of people from which the successful applicant will be chosen.

Answers

1. things like that don't really bother me

2. It's not the end of the world

3. don't let it get you down

4. there's nothing you can do about it

---

4 | Practice

Use the photo to ask students if this sort of thing can be seen in their own towns or cities, why it happens and if it annoys them or not. You could also ask them to tell you about the dirtiest/cleanest city they have ever been to. Would they prefer to live in a dirty, but lively city, or a clean, but culturally dead, city?

Read through the things in the list 1–7 with the students, helping them with the meaning of any unfamiliar vocabulary. Have them think about the list for a few minutes before discussing the items in pairs. Find out what the class thinks are the most annoying things in the list and follow up with a whole-class discussion about how to prevent these things from happening. Ask students if there are any other annoying things that they have to put up with.

5 Free practice

This exercise practises some more complaining expressions. Model and practise the pronunciation of these expressions, especially the stress and intonation patterns. Then students can complete the sentence starters. If any of them need help, refer them to the pictures for some ideas. Before they go around complaining to other people in the class, remind them or elicit from them what they can say if they want to agree. For example:

Oh, I know what you mean.
It's a pain in the neck, isn't it?
It bugs me, too.

6 More expressions with *bother*

Bother occurs in several expressions common in spoken English. Have students work in pairs matching the two halves of the dialogues. Then have them go back and underline each expression with *bother*. Ask if there are any expressions where *bother* doesn't mean *worry*. Where does *bother* mean *trouble*? (*Oh, it's no bother at all.*) Where does it mean *interrupt*? (*Sorry to bother you.*) Which expression means *I don't feel like doing something*? (*I can't be bothered.*) Which expressions mean *Don't make the effort to do something*? (*I wouldn't bother if I were you, Why bother?*)

Practise the pronunciation of the phrases and then have students memorise the expressions. They can then test each other. Remind students to record these expressions in their notebooks along with a translation.

Answers

1. f.   2. g.   3. a.   4. h.   5. d.   6. e.   7. b.   8. c.

7 Idioms focus

The idioms here describe problem situations. Have students work in pairs using their dictionaries when necessary. The meaning of the idioms should be clear from the dialogues, but having students come up with other examples helps reinforce their understanding.

Answers

1. Yes, poor guy. It's a vicious circle, isn't it?
2. It's a Catch 22 situation, isn't it?
3. Yes, and that's just the tip of the iceberg.
4. It's a bit of a mixed blessing, isn't it?

8 Speaking

Have students discuss this with a partner. You could give them an example based on your own experiences to get them started.

Unit overview

General topic
Plans, hopes and aspirations.

Dialogue
Rachel and Nick talk about their plans after leaving college.

Reading
Max is dreading meeting someone he met in an online chat room because he's been a little 'economical with the truth'.

Language input
- Starting with *what*: *What I really need to do is … , What I was thinking of is …* .
- Expressions to talk about future plans: *I can't see myself staying there for much longer, I just take things as they come*, etc.
- Sentence starters for talking about specific plans: *I might try and … , I really want to …* , etc.
- Sentence adverbs: *basically, realistically, ideally*, etc.
- Expressions to talk about plans using *if*: *if all else fails, if all goes well*, etc.

Language strip

Have students choose any expressions they find interesting and, on their own, find out more about them. In a later class, ask them to share the information. For a small group activity, ask them to find expressions that could answer the question *What are your plans for the future?* Then ask them to choose any expressions they think they might actually say themselves and explain their choices. You might need to explain some of the following expressions:

- If you're *happy doing what you're doing*, you are satisfied with your life/job/family life, etc. as it currently is. For example: *I don't plan on looking for another job; I'm happy doing what I'm doing.*
- If you *haven't got a clue*, you have no idea about the answer to a question. For example:
  A: *What are you going to write about?*
  B: *Haven't got a clue!*
- You say *Just do it* to tell someone to stop thinking about whether something is a good idea or not and to just do it. For example: *Don't worry about how much the course costs. Just do it!*
- If you just *take things as they come*, you are easy-going and don't worry about what problems might occur in the future. For example: *I'm not too bothered about what I'll be doing in five years' time. I'll just take things as they come.*

- You use *if all else fails* to say that you will do something as the last resort. For example: *If all else fails, I'll move back in with my parents.*
- If someone *wants to change the world*, they are idealistic in their wish to make a big contribution to changing society. For example: *When I was younger, I used to think I could change the world. Now I'm more of a pessimist.*
- If you say you're *in a rut*, you feel that you are doing the same thing every day and that there are no prospects for any change to make things better. For example: *I feel like I'm stuck in a rut at work.*

Remind students to record any of the expressions that they like in their notebooks.

Lead in

You can lead in to this unit by asking some general questions about the future. Write the questions on the board and explain what they mean if necessary. Here are some examples:
What do you see yourselves doing in five years?
What do you see me doing in five years?
Do you worry about what the future holds?
Do you take things as they come or do you like to plan ahead?

Listening

1 Optimistic about the future?

Before getting students to agree or disagree with the statements, ask if they think the world is generally a better or worse place today than it was when they were children. Then have them look at the statements individually before they explain their ideas to a partner. After they have completed the definition of an optimist and a pessimist, they can go back and mark the statements as being either pessimistic or optimistic. Finish off by asking whether students are generally optimists or pessimists.

> **Answers**
>
> An optimist is someone who always thinks the glass is half full, while a pessimist always thinks it's half empty.
>
> Optimistic statements: 1, 3, 6, 8
> Pessimistic statements: 2, 4, 5, 7

2 Speaking

To introduce this task you could brainstorm some general things people are optimistic and pessimistic about. Write the ideas on the board, adjusting the language where necessary. Then get the students to discuss the questions in small groups, using the board for ideas if needed. When they have finished, select a few students to give their thoughts and develop this into a class discussion.

Photo opportunity

You could use the photograph at the bottom of page 132 to extend the discussion. The person in the photo gave up his job to live in trees for many months to protest against the cutting down of trees. Find out if anyone has been involved in any protest action groups. Ask students to name some protest groups or organisations (e.g. Greenpeace, Animal Liberation Front, Amnesty International). Ask if students think these types of groups really make the world a better place, or whether anyone belongs to or gives money to a particular group.

3 While you listen (Now you're talking!)

Set the scene by reading the introduction together. Then get students to read through the gapped statements 1–4 about Rachel and Nick before you play the recording. Play the recording once all the way through and ask students to just to listen. Make sure they cover the text. Ask them to discuss the answers with a partner. Play the recording again, pausing so that they have time to fill in the gaps together.

Answers

1. Nick's thinking about doing an art course, but it depends on his results.

2. He'd like to do a French course in Paris, but he probably won't have enough money.

3. Rachel wants to learn to drive and buy a car.

4. If she can find a good job, then she'll stay where she is. Otherwise, she'll probably go back to Glasgow.

Let students read the conversation to see how many gaps they can fill in from memory. Play the recording again with pauses so that they can hear and write down exactly what was said. Finally, play the recording again with students listening while reading the tapescript on page 156. The missing words are highlighted in blue. You can then have students practise reading the conversation or parts of it in pairs. You might want to talk about several expressions in the conversation. See if anyone can explain the title *Now you're talking*! which also comes

at the end of the conversation. Explain that it is said when someone has just suggested something that's very appealing. Refer students to the **Real English** note on *the Aussies*. Ask a few students if their country has any friendly rivalry with another country and if so, if there is an *affectionate* term they call each other.

4 Speaking

You will probably need to explain *on the spur of the moment*. If someone *decides to do something on the spur of the moment,* they suddenly decide to do it without any planning. For example:

A: *You didn't tell us we were going to have class in a coffee shop today?*

B: *No, I just decided on the spur of the moment.*

This discussion probably works best in pairs first, leading to a whole-class discussion as you select a few students to share their answers.

5 Vocabulary: Phrasal verbs with *up*

Ask students if they remember some other phrasal verbs with *up* from the last unit. (e.g. *I'm going to end up having … , completely messed up, I can't put up with it any more*). As you are checking their answers, you may need to explain some of these expressions:

- If someone *turns up out of the blue*, he/she arrives unexpectedly.

- If someone *hangs up on you,* they put the phone down while you are speaking to them.

- If you *do up your flat a bit*, you fix things, do some decorating, etc.

- If you *put someone up for the night,* you give them somewhere to sleep in your house.

Remind students that they can add the phrasal verbs from this exercise to their notebooks under the heading of *up*.

Answers

1. turned 2. hung 3. do 4. come 5. cheer 6. beat
7. bottling 8. put

---

6 Speaking

Use these questions to reinforce the expressions from **5 Vocabulary: Phrasal verbs with *up*.** You can add additional questions. For example:
Talk about a time when someone just turned up out of the blue.

If a telemarketer phones you, do you talk to them or do you just hang up?

How could we do up this classroom, or this school?

If I came to stay with you, where would you put me up?

Using grammar

1 Starting with *what*

These expressions are very common in spoken English. They have the effect of focusing attention on what comes next. In more formal presentations and speeches, they often help to 'buy time' while the speaker is thinking about how to say something. For example:
What I'm going to be talking about today is … .

Model the three example sentences for students, letting them hear which words are stressed. Then have them practise saying the expressions themselves. Point out the difference between *really need to,* which expresses that it is necessary; *would really like to,* which expresses that you want to do it; and *I was thinking of doing,* which expresses that it is something you're considering. Students may wonder whether *to* should be repeated (e.g. *… is to get away, … is to learn to drive*). You can explain that adding *to* is perfectly acceptable but is not necessary.

Here students put the *what* expressions into more of a context. Have students work individually and compare their answers in pairs. They can then practise saying the expressions to each other.

Answers

1. What I really need to do is (to) learn/start learning Japanese.
2. What I'd really like to do is (to) buy a flat in the next couple of years.
3. What I really need to do is (to) start saving.
4. What I was thinking of doing is travelling around India.
5. What I'd really like to do is (to) start a family as soon as I get married.
6. What I was thinking of doing is going abroad for Christmas this year.

When students have finished, draw their attention to several collocations and expressions in the prompts: *in the next couple of years, desperately need to, in the not-too-distant future, as soon as (you) get married, go abroad.* Add other related collocations such as *in the distant future, in the near future.* Remind students to add these to their notebooks.

2 Speaking

Here students form personalised examples using this structure. As they are doing the exercise, go around, helping when necessary, especially with the word order. Before having students share their ideas with a partner, tell them how you would complete these sentences yourself and encourage them to ask you questions. Tell them to add these more personalised examples to their notebooks. Refer them to the **Grammar commentary, G31 Starting with *what*** on page 166 to review this structure.

Using vocabulary

1 Plans for the future

This exercise focuses on several expressions to respond to questions about your future plans in an unspecific way. Have students complete the sentences and compare their answers with a partner. Then model the expressions, paying attention to the stress and intonation patterns. Get students to repeat them after you. To help students remember the expressions, write the words in the box on the board and then ask different students to try and recall the whole expressions without looking at their Coursebooks. Get them to translate these expressions into their own language.

The short dialogues reinforce the meaning of the expressions by providing contexts. Once students have completed the gaps, they should practise reading the dialogues in pairs. You may need to explain that if you are *a laid-back kind of person,* you stay calm and don't let things worry you too much. You should also draw your students' attention to a couple of common questions in these dialogues:
So, how's it all going?
So, are you still off to … ?

Answers

a. perfectly happy

b. change

c. see myself

d. wait and see

e. take things

f. can't really

1. e. I just take things as they come

2. b. My plans change fairly often

3. c. I can't see myself staying there for much longer

4. a. I'm perfectly happy doing what I'm doing

5. d. I'll just have to wait and see what happens

6. f. I can't really say yet. It all depends

Finish off by asking students to think about whether they would use, or would have used in the past, any of these expressions themselves.

2 | Collocations

The sentence starters here are examples of more specific responses to questions about future plans. Explain that students should find two endings for each sentence starter. When students have finished and you have checked their answers, tell them to complete a few of the starters in ways that are true for them. Ask them to share their ideas with a partner. Also, draw students' attention to these collocations: *find a new job, going back to university, spend a bit more time with my girlfriend.*

Answers

1. a new job/somewhere nicer to live

2. abroad/back to university

3. studying/with my girlfriend

4. my own country/where I grew up

5. the world/my family

6. house/south

7. reading/sport

8. to buy a flat/for a DVD player

9. a better laptop/a new car

A fun way for students to practise these 'planning structures' is with a card game. You will need thirty-six small cards.

- Write each of the expressions in the boxes onto eighteen of the cards.

- Write two sets of the nine sentence starters on the remaining eighteen cards.

- Spread the cards out, face down on a table. The students sit around the table and take turns selecting any two cards and seeing if they match to make a complete 'planning structure' as in the exercise above.

- If they don't match, they put the cards back in the same place and the next person picks up cards. If the cards do match, the student says the complete expression, keeps the cards, and has another go.

- The winner is the person who collects the most cards.

3 | Speaking

One approach to this discussion exercise is to get students to put 1–6 in order, from most to least appealing. They could then justify their choices with a partner or in small groups. You could put some useful expressions on the board:
I'd love to …
I'd quite like to …
I could imagine working/going/sailing, etc.
I could see myself working/going sailing, etc.
That's not my cup of tea, really.
That's not my sort of thing, really.

Use the photographs to help explain any of the items in the list.

Reading

1 | Before you read

This exercise focuses more on the emotional side of the future. After students complete the matching task, get them to talk about their hopes and dreams in pairs. Draw their attention to several of the collocations here: *end up on my own, unbearably hot, back home, maybe one day, once I graduate.*

Answers

1. b.   2. a.   3. g.   4. f.   5. c.   6. e.   7. d.

2 | While you read (Economical with the truth!)

Explain to the class that they are going to read an e-mail from someone who is dreading something. You could also explain that the title, *Economical with the truth*! is a euphemism for not being totally honest, basically, for lying. Ask the class to predict some possible scenarios based on the title before asking them to read.

Answers

Max is dreading meeting Foxy, a woman he's met in a chat room, because he's told her that he's older than he really is, he's got a good job, and has his own flat in town.

When students have finished reading and have answered the question, ask them to reread the article and underline any interesting expressions or collocations. For example:

concrete plans

everything's a bit up in the air

stuck at home

right in the centre of town

3 Speaking

Get students to work in pairs discussing the situation Max has put himself in, then extend the discussion to include the topics of chat rooms and being 'economical with the truth'. You might want to brainstorm a list of situations where not being entirely honest is perhaps justifiable. For the writing task or the role play, give the class a list of expressions that could be useful:

It's your own fault.

I'd just not show up.

Don't worry about it … it'll be a bit of a laugh.

You're a bit shorter than I was expecting.

You're a bit young, aren't you?

I haven't been entirely honest with you.

Can we still be friends?

4 Language development

This exercise focuses on 'sentence adverbs' – adverbs that refer to a complete statement rather than a verb, adjective or other adverb. The ones here occur frequently in conversations about future plans. Point out that the endings of *realistically* and *basically* are generally pronounced /kli/. Practise the pronunciation of all the words before students do the matching exercise.

Answers

1. e.   2. d.   3. b.   4. a.   5. c.

Max used *hopefully* and *basically* in his e-mail.

In the personalisation task, give your own example for number 1 before students complete their sentences. Walk around the class checking and helping them with any difficulties, especially with the form of the verb after the sentence starter.

Using grammar

1 *if-* expressions

The various structures that were discussed in Unit 7 (*I'll, going to*, the present continuous and the present simple) provide just the basis for talking about the future. Students also need phrases to express, for example, attitude, certainty, uncertainty, and contingency. The expressions here all use *if*. Have the class practise saying these expressions after they have underlined them. Then get them to sort the expressions into those which are optimistic (*if all goes well, if everything goes according to plan*) and those which are pessimistic (the rest of the expressions). You might need to talk about how *should* can be used to express what you expect to happen:

She should be here by five or six this evening.

I'll just connect these bits and then it should work.

Answers

1. goes   2. goes   3. falls   4. fails   5. goes   6. work

The *if-* expressions are:

1. if all goes well
2. if everything goes according to plan
3. if that falls through
4. if all else fails
5. if nothing goes wrong
6. if that doesn't work

Draw students' attention to the **Real English** note on *Touch wood*. Ask them for equivalent expressions in their own language. You could talk about other superstitions concerning bad luck (e.g. walking under ladders, smashing a mirror) as well as superstitions concerning good luck (e.g. throwing salt over the left shoulder, crossing fingers). Extend the discussion by asking whether students have any personal superstitions, like a lucky charm or lucky piece of clothing.

20 | The world of work

Unit overview

General topic
The world of work.

Reading
Work and working conditions.

Reading
Two casual workers win the right to the same benefits as full-time employees.

Language input

- Vocabulary for talking about work conditions: *sick pay, maternity leave, contract,* etc.
- Expressions with *work* and *job: You made a really good job of it, I've been up to my eyes in work,* etc.
- Questions to ask about someone's job: *How are things at work? What are the hours like?* etc.
- Vocabulary to describe a boss: *She's very approachable, He spends the whole time sitting at his desk,* etc.
- Future continuous: *I'll be doing some work in your area tomorrow, so I'll pop in and say hello.*

Language strip

Have students choose any expressions they find interesting and, on their own, find out more about them. In a later class, ask them to share the information. For a small group activity, ask them to find expressions which are questions (e.g. *What do you do exactly?*) and come up with possible answers, or to come up with possible questions that prompt some of the expressions as answers (e.g. *It's enough to live on*). You might need to explain some of the following expressions:

- *A perk of the job* is an extra benefit that you get from your job. For example: *Getting cheap air tickets is one of the perks of working for an airline.*
- If you describe someone as *a real slave-driver,* you think they make your work really hard. For example: *I'm not too happy about having him as our new manager. I've heard he can be a bit of a slave-driver.*
- If a job *pays peanuts,* the pay is very low. You can use the expression *If you pay peanuts, you get monkeys* to say that you won't get good quality employees if the pay you offer is low.

- You would probably say *It's enough to live on* if someone asked you about your salary. It shows that it's not too low, but not that good either. For example:
  A: *So, what's the pay like at your new job?*
  B: *It's enough to live on.*
- If you say *Stress? You don't know the meaning of the word,* you are implying that the person really doesn't have a job with a lot of pressure. For example:
  A: *I hear Bob's got a lot of stress in his new job.*
  B: *Stress? He doesn't know the meaning of the word.*
- If you are *rushed off your feet,* you are very busy. For example: *I can't talk now; I'm rushed off my feet.*

Remind students to record any of the expressions that they like in their notebooks.

Lead in

Ask students if they remember the expression *working conditions,* which they met in the role play in Unit 17. Ask them what sort of *working conditions* are important to them and write these on the board. For example:
friendly atmosphere
friendly superiors
good pay

You can then go straight on to **I What do you look for in a job?**

Reading

1 | What do you look for in a job?

Go through the list, checking that students understand the expressions, for example, *flexi-time, company car* and *sick pay.* Ask individuals to rank the ideas and to then talk about them with a partner. Finish off by discussing the list as a class and coming up with the five most important aspects of a job. Point out the following collocations in the exercise for students to record in their notebooks:
work flexi-time/from home
get holiday/sick pay
earn a good salary
stuck behind a desk
do something useful

2 Before you read

This exercise gives students some more expressions connected with working conditions. Get them to work on their own first, and then compare their answers in pairs. Encourage students to use their dictionaries. Ask further questions while checking the answers. For example:

Is paternity leave common in your country?

Are companies legally obliged to give maternity leave?

What's the income tax rate in your country?

Are there industrial tribunals where you can go if you've been unfairly treated/dismissed?

How many weeks paid holiday is typical in your country?

Again, there are many useful collocations here for students to underline and record:

take maternity leave
given a proper contract
get sick pay
income tax starts at/goes up to
unfairly treated
work full-time
get three weeks' paid holiday a year
get lots of benefits
a company pension
private health insurance

Answers

1. maternity leave 2. paid holiday 3. sick pay
4. Income tax 5. unfairly treated 6. full-time
7. contract 8. lots of benefits

3 While you read (We can work it out.)

Have students read about *casual work* in the introduction and then ask them to give you some examples (e.g. *working in a bar, picking fruit, stacking supermarket shelves*). Then go through the questions, explaining the expressions *take their employers to court,* and *the implications of the decision.* Tell students to read the article to find the answers to the three questions. They can then discuss their answers in pairs.

Answers

1. Because they were denied benefits normally given to full-time workers.
2. The judge decided the women had the right to the same benefits as the other employees.
3. Other casual workers can fight for benefits from their employers as well as appeal if they are sacked unfairly.

Have students reread the text, underlining, asking about and recording any interesting expressions or collocations. For example, they may find the following: *magical door-opening piece of paper, land a job, be totally ripped off, become a little bit toothless, work directly for, major breakthrough.* You may need to explain that *CV* stands for *curriculum vitae*, which is a summary of your education and work experience that you submit when you apply for a job. Ask if students remember the expressions *a Catch 22 situation* from the previous unit.

4 Speaking

Have students discuss these questions in small groups. Write some collocations on the board to help them express their ideas:

treated + fairly, unfairly, really well, with respect, like a child, like part of the family

the money was good, not bad, terrible

5 Vocabulary work

This exercise helps extend students' vocabulary on the topic of work and working conditions. Have small groups come up with ideas before they discuss the questions as a class. You could also develop a discussion around the theme of trade unions by asking how influential trade unions are in the students' country/countries, whether students think unions are a good idea, etc.

Answers

Suggested answers:

1. A *full-time worker* works a full week; a *part-time worker* works only part of the week; a *casual worker* is employed only when there is work to be done and may work full-time or part-time during that period.
2. People *get sacked* usually when their work or behaviour is not good enough for the employer.
3. *Getting sacked* happens for the reason given above. *Being made redundant* is when the company reduces the number of workers to save money or because there is not enough work.
4. On your *CV* you include details of your education, work experience, and other skills relevant to the field you want to work in.
5. Answers will vary, but in the UK some unions are UNISON (public sector workers), TGWU (transport and general workers), CWU (communication workers) and NUT (teachers).

Using vocabulary

1 *Work* or *job*?

You could lead in by asking students to think of five adjective collocations each for the nouns *work* and *job*, and write them on the board. For example:
hard, tiring, heavy, light, physical + work
good, bad, decent, boring, well-paid + job

Then have students work in pairs on the exercise, using a dictionary to help. Check that they understand some of the more idiomatic expressions:

- If something is *hard work*, it is difficult.
- If you *make a good job out of something*, you do the job well.
- You say *It's more than my job's worth*, if someone asks you to do something at work which you are not really allowed to do, and you don't want to take the risk of getting caught.
- If you are *up to your eyes in work*, you are very busy.

> **Answers**
>
> 1. work 2. job 3. work 4. job 5. work 6. job 7. job
> 8. work

2 Speaking

Use the questions to provide practice in using some of the expressions from **1 *Work or job?*** Have small groups of students come up with some ideas and then have them share these with the class as a whole.

Listening

1 Before you listen

Ask students to tell you what each of the jobs are in the pictures on pages 140 and 141. Then get them to discuss in pairs whether they would ever like to do these jobs, what the jobs involve, and whether they could do them. Refer students back to the expressions on page 38 in Unit 5 for useful expressions.

> **Answers**
>
> a. a joiner (makes wooden frames, cupboards etc.)
> b. a smith c. a chemist d. a plumber e. a sculptor
> f. a street-sweeper

2 While you listen

Explain to students that they will hear three people talking about their jobs. Ask them to listen for phrases to help them decide what job each person does. Play the recording twice before having pairs discuss their answers. Ask them to recall the expressions that helped them decide. Then play the recording again, while students follow the tapescript on page 156.

> **Answers**
>
> 1. a chemist (*prepare all the prescriptions, keep a check on all the drugs, give advice to people who come in with minor problems, selling things over the counter, other times I feel like a doctor*)
> 2. a joiner (*working with wood, turning it into something useful*)
> 3. a street-sweeper (*somebody's got to do it, if you dropped something, they just drop everything, you name it, I've picked it up, I'd never work indoors*)

Using vocabulary

1 How are things at work?

There are many typical questions and answers for asking and talking about work. These question and answer pairings are almost as fixed as the exchange:
A: *Hello, how are you?*
B: *Fine, thanks.*

Students should be encouraged to learn typical questions and answers as whole conversations. In this exercise, there are three answers to match to each question.

> **Answers**
>
> 1. c.   2. d.   3. e.   4. b.   5. a.

After students have done the matching exercise, get them to cover up the questions, and then in pairs take turns trying to remember the questions using the answers as memory prompts. Then have students practise the questions and answers as a class, paying attention to stress and intonation. Start off by letting them read the expressions in the exercise, and then encourage them to do it from memory. If students are all in work, get them to walk around the class asking and answering questions about their own jobs, using as much of the language from the exercise as possible. You can finish up by discussing whether questions about how much someone earns are appropriate in their country.

2 Role play

Explain the task and give students a few minutes to prepare their answers. Then get them to ask and answer the questions in pairs. Make it clear that students should initially use the questions from **I How are things at work?** but they may then go on to ask any other questions they can think of in order to identify the job. After doing this, they could move on to another partner and repeat the conversation using the same job.

To make this into a game, limit the amount of time (one or two minutes, depending on level) before telling students to move on to another partner. Do this several times, asking them to note down the name and the job of each partner. No job names are revealed until the end when points are awarded for correct guesses.

3 Boss jokes

Let students read the jokes while they listen to the recording. Pause after each one to allow students to react. Help with any comprehension problems. To work on stress and pausing, write the first joke on the board and play the recording. Have the class tell you where the pauses are and mark them with a slash (/). Then play the recording again and ask students to tell you which words were stressed and underline them. Play the second joke at least twice, with students marking the pauses first and then the stress. Then go over the answers. Do the same with the third joke before having students practise reading the jokes in pairs.

4 The ideal boss

Ask if any students are, or ever have been, bosses. You could also introduce the following expressions and ask students to record them:

I'm my own boss.
I'm responsible to …
I'm responsible for …

Then have students choose two endings for each response. You might need to explain some of the following:

- Someone who is *domineering* or *dictatorial* tries to control people and order them about.
- Someone who is *approachable* is friendly and easy to talk to.
- If you *get on to someone about something*, you frequently tell them to do it – in a way that annoys them!

Answers

I. f.   2. g.   3. a.   4. h.   5. c.   6. b.   7. d.   8. e.

Students who work could then tell each other a bit about their positions in their place of work. If you want to, you could extend the work on the word *boss* by giving them expressions like:

He bosses me around.
She can be quite bossy.

5 Speaking

Give students a few minutes to look through the sixteen sentences in **4 The ideal boss** before telling a partner if any of them could be used about a boss they work (or have worked) for.

Then ask larger groups of three or four students to discuss the questions. Check as a class who students think would be the best boss, and then decide what special boss-like responsibility they can have for the rest of the class. Finish up by doing some vocabulary building for the names of different kinds of bosses.

Answers

The boss of a school is *a head teacher*.
The boss of a department is *a manager* or *head*.
The boss of a football team is *a manager*.
Other names of bosses include *chief executive officer, director, chief, commander* and *general.*

Using grammar

1 Future continuous

The future continuous is often used to describe events in the future that we see as being already fixed or decided. It often implies that we see these actions as part of a routine. Maybe a good example to illustrate this is the expression *We'll be cruising at a height of 30,000 feet* that pilots typically use when announcing the flight plan. Note that with this meaning, the verb does not necessarily have to be extended in time. For example:

They'll be starting school this autumn.
I'll be going back to Japan.

Have students do the matching task and check their answers.

Answers

1. e.   2. f.   3. a.   4. b.   5. d.   6. c.

Ask students which action the speaker sees as more important (the one in the *so* clause) and which as the background (the verb in the future continuous form). Then read the **Grammar commentary, G32 Future continuous** on page 166 together. Write the pattern *I'll be -ing, so ...* on the board and tell students to record a few examples from this page in their notebooks.

2 Grammar in context

This exercise contextualises the earlier expressions.

Answers

1. I'll be going back to Japan in the autumn, so I'll try and get you a cheap Walkman, shall I?
2. I'll be doing some work in your area tomorrow, so I'll pop in and say hello if I get the chance.
3. I'll be writing my MA thesis all summer, so I'll be working in the library a lot.
4. I'll be doing a computer course in April, so I'll be an expert on the Internet.
5. I'll be going down to my dad's next Saturday, so don't try and call me until Sunday night.
6. I'll be passing your front door, so it's no trouble giving you a lift.

After checking the answers, students should practise the short dialogues with a partner. Remind them to use the contracted form *I'll* and practise this if necessary.

3 Career plans

This is a chance for students to put some of the language from this unit into practice. Explain the task to the students. Remind them of the different language they could use from the previous unit (e.g. *What I was thinking of doing is ... , I might try and ... , If all goes according to plan*) as well as from this unit (future continuous, work vocabulary). Give them a few minutes to prepare before letting them mingle. Note that the examples of the future continuous in this exercise express an action already in progress at a certain time in the future (ten years from now): *I'll be living in a huge house*.

Finally

Assuming you and your students have completed all twenty units of *Innovations upper-intermediate*, this is the time to review the success of the course and give students advice on how to continue their English learning on their own. Here are some of the questions you could ask:

How does this course compare with other courses you have studied?

How do you feel your spoken English has improved?

How has this course changed your ideas about how English is learned?

What will you do to continue your learning?

Review: Units 17-20

The exercises here can be used as a quiz. **4 Speaking** and **6 Look back and check: More expressions with** *bother*, however, are better done as a discussion in pairs.

1 Tenses

Answers

1. haven't fixed 2. was being redecorated 3. have to be paid 4. they'd 5. I'll be seeing 6. was going to be 7. is going to be built 8. goes 9. should've been widened 10. I'll be back

2 Multiple choice

Answers

1. b. 2. a. 3. a. 4. a. 5. c. 6. a. 7. a. 8. a.

3 Second conditionals

Answers

1. would be, left
2. would be, banned, pedestrianised
3. would be, collected
4. would be, brought
5. would be, didn't charge, would get
6. would be, had

4 Speaking

Answers will vary.

5 Conversation

Answers

1. a. 2. c. 3. f. 4. b. 5. d. 6. e.

6 Look back and check: More expressions with *bother*

Answers will vary.

7 Expressions

Answers

1. don't let it get you down
2. I know what you mean
3. just doing what I'm doing
4. if everything goes according to plan
5. wait and see

8 Collocations

Answers

1. h. 2. f. 3. b. 4. a. 5. g. 6. c 7. d. 8. e.
9. j. 10. i. 11. n. 12. q. 13. k. 14. l. 15. r.
16. m. 17. p. 18. o.

9 Real English

Answers

1. e. 2. d. 3. a. 4. f. 5. b. 6. c.

10 Idioms

Answers

1. g. 2. e. 3. a. 4. j. 5. b. 6. c. 7. h. 8. d.
9. f. 10. i

11 What can you remember?

Answers will vary.

12 Vocabulary quiz

Answers

1. Nothing.
2. A building, part of a town.
3. They are not nice.
4. *Flexi-time* means there are no set start and finish times to the day; *full-time* means working a full working week; *part-time* means working only part of a week.
5. No, they are always telling you what to do.
6. No.
7. No.
8. When she's just had a baby.
9. They get paternity leave.
10. You get on with them.
11. Complaints, enquiries, phone calls.
12. Deal with them.
13. Australia – Canberra, Bulgaria – Sofia, Chile – Santiago, South Africa – Cape Town
14. Answers will vary. An example is: When I'm depressed, I eat chocolate. That makes me fat. The fatter I get, the more depressed I get, and so on.
15. If you have been unfairly treated at work or unfairly sacked.
16. To the side of the road if you're having car trouble.
17. The donkey work.
18. The local council.
19. Answers will vary. Examples are: people you don't like, the amount of work you have to do.
20. The inner city can be a rough part of town. The city centre is geographically the centre of the city and where most important offices are located.

Learner advice: The authors speak!

Answers will vary.